THE FERGIE LEGACY

A former Fleet Street journalist and BBC broadcaster, Bernard Bale is the author of 16 other books, including biographies of Craig Brown and Billy Bremner.

THE
FERGIE LEGACY

BERNARD BALE

ONE MAN'S EXTRAORDINARY IMPACT
ON BRITISH FOOTBALL

MAINSTREAM
PUBLISHING
EDINBURGH AND LONDON

First published in Great Britain in 2006 by
MAINSTREAM PUBLISHING COMPANY (EDINBURGH) LTD
7 Albany Street
Edinburgh EH1 3UG

ISBN 1 84018 992 4

A catalogue record for this book is available
from the British Library

Typeset in Ellington and Gill Sans

Printed in Great Britain by
William Clowes Ltd, Beccles, Suffolk

With thanks to Sir Alex Ferguson for countless great football moments, and with gratitude to fellow journalist Jack Webster for his words of encouragement.

CONTENTS

INTRODUCTION

WHEN YOU CONSIDER THE THOUSANDS OF PEOPLE WHO HAVE BEEN INVOLVED IN football since it became a professional sport in the nineteenth century, it is quite an achievement to become one of the few to make a real mark on the history of the game. Sir Alex Ferguson is one of those rare individuals – a living legend whose fame is not limited to Britain but has spread throughout the world.

Success on the pitch has made Fergie famous, but his background and character have made him the man he is. He has always worn his heart on his sleeve, demonstrating an unrivalled passion for football. He loved to play the game and still does, though he now joins the fray by prowling the touchline, experiencing the ups and downs of the sport vicariously through his players.

As he draws ever nearer to the end of his spectacular career, an obvious question springs to mind: what has been Fergie's long-term contribution to the game? In order to answer this question, Ferguson is put under the microscope, and his relationships with those who have been close to him are analysed. By looking at the success that Sir Alex has achieved, and by attempting to understand the reasons for this success, it is possible to come to a greater understanding of the man and his place in the game.

Ferguson has done so much in his career, especially at Old Trafford and Pittodrie. Aberdeen fans still lament losing him to Manchester United and treat him like a messiah every time he returns to the north of Scotland. If there was news of his permanent return, the whole Granite City would celebrate. And the Manchester United fans have much to be thankful to him for. Without him it is questionable whether the club would have become the force that it is today.

However, Sir Alex has not achieved all that he has in isolation – there are countless others who have benefited from working alongside the most successful British manager of recent times. It is through the impact he had on his teammates in his playing days, the influence he has had on the players he has coached and nurtured, and the knowledge that he has passed on to the coaches and assistants whom he has worked with, that his legacy becomes apparent. You cannot have a lifetime of success among other people without some of your methods rubbing off. It also happened with Bill Shankly at his beloved Liverpool. But Shankly's influence is mostly confined to his own club, whereas Fergie's influence is spread far and wide: from Gordon Strachan and Alex McLeish guiding the Old Firm in Scotland to Mark Hughes and Steve Bruce locking horns in the Premiership.

Football has been good to Alex Ferguson, but, in return, he has given much and goes on giving much. He has a wealth of experience and knowledge and bequeaths it to the game through those who have had the honour of knowing him. They are all recipients of his legacy and, in turn, pass it on to others. Indeed, there are generations still to come who will no doubt benefit from his legacy to the game because so many of those who have been associated with Sir Alex have become managers and coaches themselves. It is difficult to think of another manager who has had quite the same impact or one who has seen so many of his charges go on to become the leader of men themselves. But why is this the case? What makes Fergie so special? And just who are the beneficiaries of this unique footballing legacy?

I

THE BIG KICK-OFF

LIKE OTHER MEN WHO HAVE BEEN AT THE FOREFRONT OF THEIR CHOSEN FIELDS — men such as fellow Scots James Watt, Robert Louis Stevenson, Robert Burns and Alexander Graham Bell – Alex Ferguson is more than the much-clichéd legend in his own lifetime. He is a benefactor who has bequeathed a wealth of experience and knowledge to the game. Men who have played for him or worked alongside him have all been touched and influenced by his distinct approach to football and, indeed, life itself.

But what is he really like? Well, it depends who you talk to. Just as a guide, however, the first time I ever met Sir Alex Ferguson in 1992 he swore at me. In the corridor outside the dressing-rooms at Meadow Lane, he misheard or misunderstood what I said, and his reply included a four-letter expletive which seemed wholly inappropriate as I had simply asked him, politely, what the procedure was to request a formal interview.

His response was a bit of a shock at first, especially as United had just secured a victory over Notts County, who were there at the birth of the Premiership, although didn't last very long in the top division. Peter Schmeichel, who was standing nearby giving one of my colleagues a few quotes, witnessed what had happened and raised his eyebrows in surprise. Afterwards, he spoke to me in a gentlemanly manner, and neither of us mentioned the incident involving his boss.

I decided to brave the scowl and growl, not take the first four-letter rebuff too personally and approach Ferguson again. After all, he might be the manager but I had been associated with the club for much longer than him, my first article for the Manchester United supporters' magazine having been published in the late 1960s when Fergie was still playing in Scotland. He was much more receptive the second time round and gave a civil answer. Dr Jekyll was back and Mr Hyde had disappeared.

At subsequent press conferences, I have seen him verbally assassinate a whole series of journalists with one machine-gun-like tirade; on other occasions, I have seen him be charming and witty – the life and soul of the party even. Comparisons with the split personality in Stevenson's Jekyll and Hyde story do indeed seem apt, except that Fergie does not need a potion to become a fearful character – he can do it at the drop of a hat.

The taciturn and aggressive side to the Old Trafford boss is well documented, the softer side less so. One example of Ferguson's generosity and magnanimity occurred a few years ago when I was asked if it might be possible to arrange for a boy from Jersey to be the United mascot for a home match. The boy was dying and had been a lifelong United fan. Although United's policy was not to have mascots at that time, the club made an exception for the young lad. Fergie had all the players make a fuss of him, and because the boy was in a wheelchair, he carried him onto the Old Trafford pitch. It was an act of personal kindness, and to his dying day, that boy saw Alex Ferguson as a hero.

Stories such as this leave little doubt that there are contrasting sides to Fergie's personality but what has made him the man he is? To better understand the seemingly contradictory elements of his character, it is necessary to examine his early years. Alexander Chapman Ferguson was born on 31 December 1941, making Hogmanay an even more significant date in the Ferguson household. His mother and father had been married for just six months when Alex was born. By today's standards, there is nothing special about that, but in the prim and proper world of the 1940s, conceiving out of wedlock was still something that raised eyebrows. In this way, you could say that the controversy that has shadowed Ferguson throughout his life began even before his birth.

He was named Alexander after his father, a father for whom Sir Alex has always had the utmost respect and affection. However, although his father was a strong influence in his life, he has always maintained that he inherited his rugged determination from his mother, who had all the tender maternal qualities you would hope for but was also a terrier in her approach to life and its many problems. In his autobiography *Managing My Life*, Fergie acknowledges this fact: 'Dad was the driving force but my mother had a stronger and more determined streak in her.' He also states that he inherited some of the strengths that have contributed to his success directly from his mother: '. . . my mother had incredible courage and determination, and if those qualities have helped me to succeed, I am sure I have her to thank.'

While his parents were an important influence, Ferguson and his younger brother Martin were also moulded by the area in which they grew up. The family lived in a flat over a pub in a part of Glasgow that was dominated by heavy industry and, in particular, shipbuilding. Sir Alex is very proud of his heritage and is known as Govan's most famous son.

Govan had been at the centre of the world-renowned Clydeside shipbuilding industry since the late nineteenth-century, and the small town had been incorporated into Glasgow proper as a consequence of the large influx of workers into the area. It also underwent a surge in population in the 1930s when new housing estates were built to relieve the overcrowded slums of the Gorbals. The area's strategic importance then made it a prime target for Hitler's Luftwaffe during the Second World War. In the most severe raids in 1941, over 600 people were killed and nearly 7,000 houses suffered serious damage. It was in this scarred landscape that Ferguson grew up.

Ferguson's father worked at the shipyards as a labourer, mostly helping to fit steel panels on the sides of ships. When war broke out, he was keen to fight for his country but was turned down for both the Royal Navy and the Army because he was unfit for service. He had sustained two bad factory injuries in the past, one of which had removed his right thumb. But the fact that he was unable to go to war was no doubt a relief to his wife, who would otherwise have been left on her own at home with two small boys to look after.

Nobody could ever have justifiably accused Alex Ferguson, sen., of ducking out of doing his national service because he had a great reputation locally as a man you could trust in a crisis. Few would ever cross him, and having him as a father must have opened many doors for Alex and Martin. Ferguson has referred to the fact that when he returns to Govan there are still those who refer to him as 'Alex's boy' rather than as the manager of Manchester United.

When shipbuilding went into decline after the war, it seemed quite an injustice, as Govan had contributed so much to both the First and Second World War efforts and had also steeled itself against the bombing raids of Hitler's Luftwaffe. Years earlier, the people of Govan had coped with the effects of a General Strike and

16

depression and had come through these hardships. Now, however, the decline of heavy industry hit the area hard, and Govan retained a reputation for poverty and deprivation for much of the remainder of the century. The strength of character that was demonstrated by the people of Govan to overcome the hardships after the war influenced Ferguson's approach to life, as he himself has acknowledged: 'Growing up in Govan means that you are among people who come from generations of hard workers, people who knew that they could not simply give up and do something else. You cannot grow up in an environment like that without some of their steel rubbing off on you. Govan people just don't give up.'

He and his brother went to Broomloan Road Primary School and ended up in the same year, even though Martin was a year younger. This was because Ferguson suffered a period of bad health when he was ten which saw him contract a kidney condition and also go through two hernia operations. Having been commended for his bravery during those operations, he never missed an opportunity to show off his scars as if they were some kind of duelling brand of honour.

Young Alec, as he was known then, proved to be intelligent and was prepared to work hard at what interested him at school. He did well in academic subjects, such as English and arithmetic, but also at sport. Although he took the 11+ a little later because of his health problems, he passed with flying colours and could probably have achieved good results at high school if he had been more interested. But at all school levels, sport was his priority with, of course, football top of the list and swimming not far behind. His school report cards show that he had an excellent mind but that his lack of commitment and real interest in his academic studies impeded his progress. Possibly the stigma of being held back was a problem. He has mentioned in interviews that he did not like sitting in classrooms with younger children.

He had a reputation for being able to take care of himself at school and nobody wanted to fall foul of him. He was not a bully, but he did not shrink back from a challenge or an opportunity to put right any injustice that he saw in the playground. As his teacher Liz Thomson once said, he could start a fight in an empty room, but as a general rule, he did not seek to start trouble, simply to be there on the winning side when it reached its conclusion.

In an area like Govan, you learn about life quite early on, and the two boys frequently witnessed the devastating results of over-drinking and violence. Living as they did over a pub meant that their bedroom window was a prime spot from which to watch the inevitable fights that erupted at least once a week in the street outside. Perhaps it was here that the famous Fergie fighting spirit was sharpened, or perhaps it was here that he learned when to duck and when to get one over on his opponent. Such things were important to a lad growing up in Govan. The chances of going without at least one close encounter of the fisticuffs kind were pretty slim, and Alec and Martin were also witnesses to gang warfare and some of the society-splitting bigotry of religious differences.

In the sanctuary of their own home, however, none of that existed. It might be assumed that Sir Alex must be a die-hard Protestant like so many in the area – especially as he is a Rangers fan – but the situation was not quite as straightforward as that. His father was indeed a Protestant, but his mother was a Catholic. However, it was agreed that young Alec would be raised as a Protestant, which meant that he was among the majority of Govan's faithful. With a Protestant father and a Catholic mother, the Ferguson boys learned from a young age that people from different religious backgrounds can coexist harmoniously, and Sir

Alex has fully backed attempts to rid sport of sectarianism and racism.

The brothers also learned early on about the importance of football. Govan looks as if it is simply one small part of Glasgow, but it is very much its own area with its own heritage and sense of community. Football has been a major part of that heritage for many years. An amateur side called Lancefield began playing in Govan in 1864, three years before the birth of Queens Park – which lays claim to being one of the oldest clubs in the world and still survives today – and another of the area's clubs, Dumbreck FC, was one of the eight founding members of the Scottish Football Association. Works teams were abundant, and from 1877 Rangers played in the area at the first Ibrox Stadium before moving to the site of their current ground in 1899.

Ferguson, sen., loved his football, and it said something of the man's independent approach to life that, though he was a Protestant, he was chiefly a Celtic fan and chairman of the local branch of the supporters' club. Alec and Martin had divided loyalties. Alec took to Rangers and Martin to Celtic, although at that stage, their main love was football and the Scotland national side. Fergie has always been fervently patriotic, and it is hard to imagine him cheering on England in the World Cup. If their father did not take them to Ibrox when Rangers were at home, it was not unusual for the boys to make their own way into the ground without going through a turnstile; to complete their adventure, they would collect empty bottles and pick up the deposits of a few old pennies each as they returned them to the shops on their way home.

While Ferguson loved watching football, the greatest thrill came from taking part and scoring goals, and playing the game was the favourite pastime of young Alec and Martin. The two boys spent many a happy hour in each other's company, both indoors and out, banging a ball about, and their father regularly took them to the park and coached them in the basic skills of football, insisting that they work hard and practise. He would have been appalled by the time spent by young players today rehearsing goal celebrations. This coaching proved very beneficial to Alec in particular, who learned the basic art of football and the benefits of being equally strong with both feet.

When it came to organised football, the junior school did not have its own team, so Alec had to look elsewhere for regular games. In 1950, he started to play for the local company of the Boys' Brigade, which had a decent team. He soon proved himself to be a star goal scorer, but his father did not believe in overdoing praise and ensured that he kept his son's feet firmly on the ground by pointing out the aspects of his play that needed improvement.

Alec progressed with the Boys' Brigade team and remained with it into his secondary-school days. And his connection to the organisation has continued throughout the years: he is now its honorary vice-president. 'I learned many of the basic skills of life through the Boys' Brigade and some of the skills were invaluable as a professional footballer and as a manager,' he said. 'I think it is good for young people to get involved in such organisations, because they teach you about discipline and helping others.'

After the Boys' Brigade, Alec joined Harmony Row, a kind of social club for the young. It was the football team which attracted him, but he also proved to be a dab hand at snooker. At the age of 15, he could take on and beat anyone in the club, even those who were some years older than him. In 1956, after two seasons playing for Harmony Row, he was spotted and snapped up by Drumchapel Amateurs. He was now entering more elite company. Many big football names, from Archie Gemmill to Mo Johnston, have played for the Drumchapel club, as well as one of today's top young managers, David Moyes. They all appear on the club's roll of honour, where the name of Alex Ferguson can also be clearly seen, a reminder of his days as a bustling, goal-scoring forward.

He continued to play for Harmony Row and also turned out for Govan High School, so there was no shortage of football for the teenage Alex Ferguson. He also played for Glasgow Schools and eventually for the Scottish Schools team. One of his teammates at the time was Craig Brown, and the two men would share many football memories during the years to follow. 'I remember him well,' Brown told me. 'He was a good guy to have on your side, because he was always prepared to get stuck in where it hurt. He was a good ball player with great two-footed skills. If he had a flaw, it was his reluctance to pass the ball if there was a remote chance of going for glory. He was a typical old-fashioned forward, though, and could use both feet, head, elbows, knees, the lot.'

At the age of 16, Alex Ferguson had to make a decision. He could not stay at school, because academically he was not really getting the right results, and although he wanted a career in football, there did not seem to be a rush of full-time professional clubs offering him a place. It looked like he would have to find a job.

Any position had to be in or near Govan so that he remained in the environment that he knew best, but Alex steered clear of the shipyards. Instead, he accepted a five-year apprenticeship with a company named Wickman Lang, a toolmaking company on the nearby Hillington Industrial Estate. He learned all the skills of the trade and attended a day-release course at a local college to add theory to his practical education.

But even as he joined the firm, it was already struggling for survival, and the apprenticeship did not last the planned five years at Wickman's. Ferguson was into his second year of the apprenticeship when the company folded due to financial difficulties. He could have simply been cast aside, but instead he was helped by the firm's manager, Jimmy Malcolm, who arranged for his debenture to be transferred to Remington Rand on the same industrial estate. Thus Ferguson continued to learn the toolmaking trade while his heart was really in another.

Trade unions were gathering strength in the 1950s, and Alex not only joined the Amalgamated Engineering Union but was as actively interested as his years and football commitments would allow. He was clearly influenced by his father's socialist leanings and twice found himself among those taking the lead in industrial action.

A few months after starting his apprenticeship, Ferguson had signed for Queens Park, a Glasgow team like no other. The club has enjoyed some memorable moments in the English FA Cup and has the honour of having Hampden Park as its home ground, but at the same time it was a minnow among giants. Queens Park was strictly an amateur club and nobody received a penny for playing, only the honour and a fantastic shop window in which to show what they could do. However, Fergie has often said that he trained harder there than anywhere else and that when you pulled on that famous hooped shirt you were expected to play as hard as any of the stars across the city at Celtic Park or Ibrox.

His football career blossomed at Queens Park, and in 1960, he joined St Johnstone, a much bigger club based in Perth. At first he opted to remain an amateur, and because he was still working for Remington, training with the club was difficult, and most of the time he had to make his own arrangements. In 1962, he joined the pro-ranks, and for the first time, Ferguson was being paid to play football, albeit on a part-time basis.

Despite this step up in his fortunes, it proved to be an unhappy four years at St Johnstone, Ferguson suffering the frustration of not being a regular first-team choice. He did, however, have his moments and was occasionally in the right place at the right time to score an all-important goal. He nearly joined Raith Rovers and Third Lanark, but it was not to be, and it took quite an earth-shattering performance to stir his career into serious action. St Johnstone were playing away to Rangers the weekend before Christmas 1963 and had adopted defensive tactics to no avail, since the team from Glasgow led 1–0 at half-time. Manager Bobby Brown told Alex to play further forward in the second half and the game was transformed. The result was a 3–2 away win for St Johnstone, and the newspapers not only screamed that it was the shock of the season but also hailed the Saints' hat-trick hero – Alex Ferguson. But even this success did not result in Fergie's name being one of the first on the team sheet.

Suddenly, Scottish football was talking about the new kid on the block who had proved to be 'Jack the giant killer' against the mighty Rangers. His face was in the newspapers, and the fact that he was still a toolmaker only added to the legend. It was his first introduction to dealing with the press – and he received very favourable treatment compared to some of his later reviews.

St Johnstone immediately put a £3,000 price tag on his head to warn off other clubs. Fergie protested, but his vociferous pleas fell on deaf ears until a deal was finally struck which took him to Dunfermline during the summer break of 1964.

Dunfermline had been tracking him for a while. Their manager Jock Stein had been impressed by Ferguson's aggression and total commitment. Even when Stein left to take over as manager of Hibernian, Dunfermline remained on the Fergie trail and finally got their man in time for the 1964–65 season. It was time for Alex to become a full-time professional footballer and he now left Remington at the age of 22, having seen out his apprenticeship. He felt some remorse about leaving his pals at the factory and actually took a cut in income at this point, having previously received payment from both St Johnstone and from Remington.

All that he had learned and experienced in his formative years began to pay dividends when Ferguson moved to Dunfermline, his game improving as he turned all his attention to the career he had wanted from the start. He got off to a flying start and impressed with a few vital goals, then hit the headlines with a hat-trick against Clyde. The Dunfermline faithful began to rate him.

His dad was obviously proud of him but still tended to highlight the negative aspects of his performances rather than focus too much on what he was getting right. Perhaps that is how one of the characteristics of Fergie's own brand of man management was honed. He has a reputation for being hard on his players, giving a pat on the back when it is deserved but not massaging any egos. In fact, the pat on the back or the 'well done, son' is a seldom-seen ray of sunshine glimpsed through the black cloud of Ferguson's everyday demeanour – a black cloud that threatens to burst into a storm at any time.

There have, of course, been other taciturn Scottish managers, such as Bill Shankly, Matt Busby and Jock Stein. They could all be tough when they had to be but few have been so frightening as Fergie in a fury. Seeing him in a rage has sent many big men running for cover. Perhaps his temper can also be traced back to his father who was known locally as someone not to be messed with. His father also had a reputation for being keen to take the side of the underdog, a personality trait Fergie himself has demonstrated at points during his Old Trafford tenure.

Dunfermline certainly provided Alex Ferguson with a bigger and better stage, and he responded accordingly. Every victory was like winning a battle and every defeat was bitterly swallowed. While others were quick to change the subject after a loss, Fergie took it personally and would brood for a while before starting to focus on the next challenge. He continues to do so to this day, taking any defeat of his team or any criticism aimed at his club to heart.

He was nothing if not passionate and took that passion onto the training ground, where it was not uncommon for him to be berated by his teammates for being overzealous. His response? Sometimes it would be simply to verbally remind them that it was a man's game, while on other occasions fists would be raised. Fergie was that kind of player: always in the thick of the action and never compromising in his confrontations. He has certainly not changed in that respect, as many opponents, referees and even his own staff would testify.

It would be best to describe him as an old-fashioned centre-forward, good in the air, lethal in the six-yard box and prepared to barge his way through any wall of defence. Much has been said about his use of elbows during his playing days, and he has never been slow to metaphorically elbow a player who did not fit in with his style of management. Alex Ferguson was not a flair player. He did not collect the ball from the halfway line and weave past several players before planting the ball in the net from 30 or 40 yards. He was a warrior, a goal poacher, cashing in on defensive errors and slippery-fingered goalkeepers.

Former Scotland manager Craig Brown was playing for Falkirk at the time and remembers playing against Ferguson: 'He was hard to play against because he was a real tough character. He never flinched no matter how hard a defender tackled him or how much a goalkeeper piled into him. He just kept plugging away. He didn't just take it though, he dished it out, too. Alex was never what you might call a dirty player, but there was more than one opposing player who had to get some raw steak for his eye after getting acquainted with Fergie's elbow.

'I saw him in action as a player, and it was no surprise that he later went into management. He loved the game and was dedicated to it. During the years we have both been in the game, I have encountered him in his role and mine as managers and also socially. He is definitely a one-off. There really is only one Alex Ferguson.'

That he might one day become a manager was obvious to all those who came into contact with him. He was one of the few players of his day who liked to ask questions about training and coaching. No matter who was in charge of the training sessions, Ferguson would want to know why certain exercises were being employed and what benefit they would have. This was not the questioning of someone who was rebelling against authority but of someone who was genuinely keen to take in information, someone with drive and ambition.

While other players were socialising with wine, women and song, Alex Ferguson was eating, sleeping and drinking football. He read all the football newspapers and magazines, constantly adding to his knowledge. He was the sort of guy you would want on your pub quiz team. No matter what the opposition, Alex Ferguson probably knew more about them than they knew themselves. This is another trait that Fergie has continued to demonstrate throughout his career and something that his many disciples will have observed about him.

He also showed that the bigger the challenge, the more he was up for the game. He revelled in matches against Celtic or Rangers and was once or twice accused of being a different and much better player when faced with opposition from either of the Old Firm teams. That was a little harsh, because human nature decrees that the tougher the opposition, the harder players will try to win.

It was during his Dunfermline days that Fergie sampled European football for the first time. The club had qualified for the 1964–65 Fairs Cup, now the UEFA Cup. Fergie came back in time from a ligament injury that season to be involved in the European run and the side travelled as far as the third round, beating Örgryte of Sweden and Stuttgart before losing 2–1 to Athletic

Club Bilbao, having taken the high-profile Spanish side to a play-off match.

Ferguson savoured those European trips, soaking up the atmosphere of both the special home games and the away matches in grounds which were far removed from those he had played at in his junior days. There was still business to be done at home, though, and Pars manager Willie Cunningham had a tough job on his hands as he steered his side to a possible League and Scottish Cup Double. In particular, he had to make a number of tough decisions concerning Ferguson. Although Fergie was the team's top scorer, the word on the street was that he was missing too many chances, chances that sometimes meant the difference between a win and a draw. There was no question that he was a better player to have on your side than against you, but he was inconsistent and he sometimes allowed his natural flair for trade-union thinking to get him involved in other people's squabbles with the management. Bobby Brown, his former boss at St Johnstone, revealed that Ferguson was a born leader, especially in the dressing-room where he would often speak up for players who were shyer than he was. 'He was almost always the first to speak up about wages,' Brown once said in a BBC Radio Scotland interview.

Dunfermline narrowly missed out on the championship in the 1964–65 season, but they did reach the Scottish Cup final. The job of putting the ball in the back of the net on such a great occasion would go to either Fergie or John McLaughlin. It was a difficult choice, but Cunningham eventually decided on McLaughlin. However, he didn't tell anyone until an hour before kick-off and therefore named his side with the whole squad present in the dressing-room at Hampden.

Fergie recounted later that his stomach was churning as he awaited news of the team selection: not because of pre-match nerves but because he had a gut feeling that he was going to be left out. In the event, he was right. Ferguson's omission was made worse by the fact that there were no substitutes in those days, so anyone not named in the starting XI had no option but to be a spectator for the duration of the game.

Fergie did not take it well. In fact, he really hit the roof and berated his boss in front of the whole team for leaving him out and for not telling him before it was announced in the dressing-room. Much water has passed under the bridge since then, but Fergie still stirs a little at the reminder of that event which was memorable for all the wrong reasons. As it was, the Pars lost the match 3–2 to Celtic. Whether the result would have been any different with Alex Ferguson in the line-up will always remain open to debate. McLaughlin scored one of the Dunfermline goals, but perhaps Fergie's presence and will to win would have made a difference.

Ferguson did learn an important lesson that day, as he later explained during an interview with sportswriter Jack Webster: 'It happens to a lot of players that they miss out on a big occasion when they at least half-expect to be playing. Managers have tough decisions to make sometimes, but it is only fair on the players to be disappointed to tell them on a one-to-one basis before the decision is made common knowledge. I have always tried to do that and not let them go through the anguish and embarrassment that I once experienced.'

Ferguson requested a transfer after the cup final but was refused, and he actually went on to have a really good 1965–66 season, finishing as the top scorer in Scotland as Dunfermline once again went close to winning a cabinet full of silverware. However, despite his good form, he again sought the exit door at the end of the season but was given a pay rise instead.

More money was not a bad consolation because Alex Ferguson had taken a very large stride in his personal life in March 1966 –

he got married. He met Cathy Holder at the Locarno dance hall in 1965, after having first seen her at a Remington Rand strike meeting, and far from being just another girlfriend, they soon began to steady date. The wedding, a simple registry-office ceremony, was a happy occasion. Since then, the couple have enjoyed a good marriage and have been blessed with three sons: Mark, born on 18 September 1968, and twins Jason and Darren, born on 9 February 1972. It could be argued that being a father has added to Ferguson's management style. He had to learn to understand and deal with the foibles of youth, something that would hold him in good stead as he brought forth a succession of home-grown Manchester United talent that eclipsed even the legendary Busby Babes. 'You can never win anything with kids,' TV pundit and former Liverpool and Scotland star Alan Hansen once famously said – and he has been reminded of it ever since. Alex Ferguson proved him wrong by encouraging and cajoling his 'kids' to the championship in 1995–96 and an amazing run of subsequent success. Admittedly, those kids of the class of '95 were aided by sixth formers Eric Cantona and Steve Bruce, but, in essence, it was a very young side with an important factor in their favour: they had a manager who knew how to get the best out of them.

To his credit, Alan Hansen has admitted that he was wrong about Manchester United that year, but, as Fergie has pointed out more than once since then, Hansen was really quite right in general but had simply underestimated the potential of the Old Trafford youngsters.

While Ferguson was experiencing significant changes in his private life, his football career was also developing. Scotland manager Bobby Brown, who had previously been Fergie's boss at St Johnstone, had been keeping an eye on his ex-player's good form. Ferguson made a step towards his senior international breakthrough when he was selected to play for the Scottish Football League against the English Football League. A regular fixture at the time, it was considered to be like an international reserves game with guest players. Today there would be little point in the fixture other than to make money, because of all the foreign players who have flooded both leagues, but back then it was an important match.

The English league won 3–0, but Ferguson did have the ball in the net only to have his goal ruled out for being offside. He was disappointed to say the least, but there must have been some consolation in being named in a Scotland squad which was to go on an epic tour in 1967 with matches in Israel, Hong Kong, Australia, New Zealand and then Canada.

In the seven matches in which he played, Ferguson scored ten goals, but there is no point in looking in the record books for his list of caps, as the Scottish Football Association decreed that this was a representative tour of friendly matches rather than a full international tour and therefore no caps were awarded to those taking part. That decision has always been a sore point for Alex Ferguson, who has mentioned the fact in subsequent interviews, and you can see his point of view when you look at caps being handed out like confetti to today's so-called international players from the home nations. A full cap continued to elude him for the rest of his playing career, and despite all the silverware and other honours that he has won, Fergie has always felt that there is something missing from his amazing collection. A professional footballer who is also such a dedicated Scot would always want to be recognised as having played in a full international for his country.

In July 1967, his career took another sudden turn when he was approached and asked if he might be interested in playing for Rangers. It was an easy decision. He was a lifelong Rangers fan brought up in an area of Rangers fans, and the thought of pulling on the famous blue shirt must have been like a dream come true. Within a couple of days, he had signed and could not help revealing his excitement to the press, telling them that he had achieved his greatest ambition. At that stage in his life, it was: he had reached his utopia. But, of course, there were many more ambitions to be realised in the years to come.

Despite Ferguson's excitement, he still had to deliver on the pitch. However, Rangers were going through a bad spell and were in the shadows of their arch-rivals Celtic, who had just become the first British club to win the European Cup. The headlines raved about the Lisbon Lions, while at Ibrox there was a kind of siege mentality taking hold.

Ferguson had been brought in to grab goals, and he did just that when he pulled on a Gers shirt for the first time in a friendly against Eintracht Frankfurt. He scored a hat-trick and was the star of the show. This meant there were now even greater expectations placed on him as Rangers started the 1967–68 season. It started well enough, and they were soon leading the table, but Ferguson entered a goal drought.

Then, in November 1967, Scott Symon, the manager who had brought Ferguson to the club, was unexpectedly sacked and replaced by Davie White, whom Symon had personally appointed as his assistant during the summer. It seemed that Rangers wanted to change their management style and have someone who was more of a training-field and tracksuit boss. Symon, who had been the man in charge when Fergie had stood on the terraces as a young teenager cheering on the team, was one of the suited old guard. Although White was the choice of the board, he was certainly not Fergie's preferred boss. In fact, he was very unhappy to see the man considered by many to be 'Mr Rangers' departing so unceremoniously and immediately handed in a transfer request, something which he did throughout his career if he did not agree with a management decision. Handing out ultimatums is one of Fergie's trademarks. He is always determined to get his own way and has found that taking such action has often been successful. Let's face it, if you have a major goal scorer or a top manager who suddenly gives you the option of doing things his way or losing him, it does clarify the situation.

On this occasion, his brinkmanship didn't work. He stayed at Ibrox and started scoring again, and it seemed that Rangers were going to win the championship, even though Celtic were breathing down their necks for much of the 1967–68 season. It was during the run-in to the title that Fergie learned another great lesson. Celtic boss Jock Stein suddenly announced that he thought Rangers were too far ahead for anyone to stop them winning the league unless Rangers themselves blew it. It was a classic mind-game tactic which not only inspired Stein's own players to prove him wrong but also placed an element of doubt in the minds of the Rangers players. At the end of the season, Celtic received the championship trophy and Rangers won nothing. Was it a coincidence that Fergie steered Manchester United to championship success when it seemed that Newcastle had virtually won the title in 1995–96? No, that was Ferguson drawing on what he had learned from Stein and ensuring that he placed the necessary mental pressure on Kevin Keegan and his players so that the Reds could snatch the league title away from them.

The following season was not any better as Ferguson found himself at odds with Rangers officials on more than one occasion, and his first-team games became fewer. However, there was an opportunity for glory when he was picked to play against Celtic in the Scottish FA Cup final in 1969, but this turned into a nightmare when the Bhoys won 4–0. Ferguson was blamed for the loss of the first goal, scored by legendary Celtic skipper Billy

McNeill. Fergie was accused of having not stopped the Celtic captain from getting his head to the ball, and the incident was even more noteworthy because McNeill rarely scored. The fact that the near post was completely unattended seemed to escape everyone's attention, and it was Ferguson who was berated by White at half-time.

In the days that followed, Ferguson's name was trailed across the media, in post-mortem style, as the main culprit for Rangers being heavily beaten on such an important occasion. In fact, he had played well for the rest of the game, and the criticism was unfair. Perhaps this could be seen as the start of Ferguson's problems with the media.

Fergie did not take it lying down, of course, and never flinched from airing his views on White. Perhaps that is why he never played in the Rangers first team again, instead being relegated to train and play with the youth team. Although his banishment was a form of public punishment, it did not really have the desired effect, as Fergie proved to be a popular and very useful member of the junior set-up and took full advantage of the situation to begin the coaching of young players. The experience proved to be another useful part of the learning process for Ferguson on his way towards a career in management.

Fergie was still a Rangers player when the 1969–70 season began, but interest from Matt Gillies, then manager of Nottingham Forest, led to an agreement between the two clubs that the player would move south. Fergie was up for it and saw a great opportunity to return to first-team football and show what he could do in the English Football League. Cathy was not so keen, though: she was already a football widow with young children and realised that she would find it even harder to cope living away from her family and friends.

The deal fell through, but Falkirk had been waiting in the

wings, and, to much surprise, Ferguson agreed to join the Second Division side. A few days later, he would have been kicking himself when Rangers parted company with Davie White. The departure of the Rangers boss could possibly have paved the way for Fergie to return to the first-team squad under the guidance of new boss Willie Waddell, who made no secret of his admiration for Fergie as a player.

Scottish football is not a large pond, and it is rare that a player joins another club without meeting some familiar faces. There were several greeting Fergie when he went to Falkirk, among them Andy Roxburgh, who was a former teammate at Queens Park. Perhaps the most significant, though, was Falkirk manager Willie Cunningham, who had previously been Ferguson's boss at Dunfermline and who had dropped him from the Scottish Cup final without pre-warning. It seemed inevitable that they would clash again, but they both knew that there was a job to be done and that, as professionals, they just had to get on with it.

The task in hand was to get Falkirk – or the Bairns as they are affectionately known – back into the top division. They had been there before and had given a good account of themselves, even though much of their success had been at Division One level. They had also lifted the Scottish Cup in 1957. Fergie's role was to partner Roxburgh up front, and they combined well to form a quite lethal strike force.

Meanwhile, Alex assumed his trade-union mantle once again when he became chairman of the Scottish Professional Footballers' Association in 1970, remaining in the position until 1973. During that time, he had just one dispute to handle and that was at his own club in response to a disciplinary decision by the manager. Players threatened to strike, but the matter was settled before it went too far, with the vociferous Fergie negotiating successfully with Cunningham.

This demonstrated another side to Fergie's character, namely that he was a man who could not sit by and let others represent him. He could never do things by proxy, and he is still the same today. If he has something to say to a player, or anyone else for that matter, he is still the shop steward who will unflinchingly wade in and put matters straight.

Falkirk were promoted at the first attempt, and the following season Fergie found himself in the line-up to face Rangers. Even though the Gers had rested a few players in preparation for a tie against Celtic, they were still tough opponents, and Falkirk were not expected to dent their pride. However, contrary to people's expectations, the Bairns won 3–1 with Fergie in the thick of things and upsetting a nervous Rangers defence enough to give his colleagues the opportunities to score. There were mixed results in other games, but Falkirk stayed afloat in the first division with Ferguson scoring a few, making a few and occasionally getting himself into trouble with referees.

Ferguson's role was changing as he neared the end of his best playing days. He was 31 and still had a few years left, but 1972 was the start of his twilight zone as a player rather than his peak. He was still a valued player, but Cunningham saw something else in him and increasingly involved him in the coaching side of things. He was also sent on spying missions to assess the strengths and weaknesses of forthcoming opponents. This increased responsibility was possibly because Ferguson was a restless spirit and continually wanted and needed new challenges. However, this also meant that when Hibernian asked about signing Ferguson, he wanted to go. Cunningham put a stop to it, and, once again, the two men were at loggerheads for a short time.

'We had many a set-to,' said Cunningham. 'We were always adult and professional, though. I never bore any grudge, and I don't think Alex did either. In fact, over the years, we have always remained friends and our families have kept in touch. That doesn't happen if you cannot respect each other's viewpoint.'

Ferguson was proving himself to be a good coach and very capable of dealing with players. Before he was officially appointed first-team coach, Falkirk were at the bottom of the league table, but after he reorganised things, the results improved and very soon the club was starting to climb out of its predicament. Such was the improvement at Falkirk that Aberdeen manager Jimmy Bonthrone considered asking Fergie to become his assistant at Pittodrie. It was not to be at that time, though; the Dons days were yet to come.

Just as things seemed to be going well at Falkirk, the player-coach carpet was tugged from under his feet with the departure of Willie Cunningham shortly before the end of the 1972–73 season. Fergie was asked to take care of team matters while a replacement was found, and it was even suggested that he might apply for the job.

It seemed like an exciting challenge, but Fergie felt that his playing days were far from over, and he was not entirely comfortable with the way the club's directors had handled matters. He did not want to jump from the frying pan into the fire. His caution seemed sensible when the directors appointed John Prentice as manager, a decision which raised many eyebrows and placed question marks against the board's understanding of the club's real needs and direction. Prentice had previously been in the Brockville hot seat but had forsaken the club to join Dundee. The fans were none too happy to see him return, and Fergie's decision not to apply for the job was a shrewd one, as he might have taken on more headaches than achievable targets.

The new manager instantly made his presence felt by taking away Fergie's coaching role. It was a short-sighted move because Alex had not only gained the respect of his fellow players and the supporters but had also added to his own knowledge by attending a coaching course during the summer at Lilleshall, a course that has spawned many of the great managers and coaches of recent years.

Another Ferguson transfer request seemed inevitable and was accepted before the start of the 1973–74 season. It was bad news for the supporters but good news for Ally MacLeod, the ever-ambitious and ever-optimistic manager of Ayr United. Alex was offered a good deal by the club, which only took on board part-timers but nevertheless made Fergie an offer he found acceptable.

Ally's optimism and Fergie's determination turned out to be a successful combination. While Falkirk struggled and were eventually relegated from Division One that season, Ayr prospered. The icing on the cake for Ferguson was scoring the winning goal against Falkirk when the Bairns visited Ayr, thus adding to the woes of John Prentice. As a part-timer, Alex was now also able to further his education outside football and had time to help a friend run a pub.

On the field, it was at this time that a few niggling injuries started to disrupt Fergie's appearances. In February 1974, he scored an excellent goal for Ayr against another of his former clubs, St Johnstone. There were many cheers and pats on the back, but had everyone known that it was to be the last senior goal of Alex Ferguson's playing career, perhaps there would also have been a standing ovation. A couple of months later, he played his last senior match when he turned out for Ayr against Falkirk. Again, it was not known that it was going to be Fergie's farewell.

Shortly after the game against Falkirk, a doctor put him through a rigorous medical, and it was discovered that he had enlarged arteries. Although he was only 32, continuing to play football at that level would possibly affect his long-term health. Had the doctor known that Fergie was going to head into management before long, he might have persuaded him to continue playing, as that probably would have put less strain on his heart.

By amicable agreement, Fergie's contract with Ayr was terminated. However, he was still a young man with a young family to support, and he needed to find an alternative source of income. The experience he had gained running the pub with his friend certainly provided him with an option, and even though his wages had never resembled the astronomic figures today's players command, he was not too badly off and could easily afford to start a small business.

But he had football experience that was way ahead of his years and contacts that could not be simply allowed to fade into memories. Above all, he still had a burning passion to succeed in football and was not ready to walk away from the game. Fergie's management days were about to begin.

2

THE BOSS

ALEX FERGUSON WAS NEVER REALLY CUT OUT TO SIMPLY RUN A PUB AND HAVE NO further hands-on interest in football, although he did get very involved in the business of being a publican when he opened his own establishment in Govan called Fergie's. He put his usual unswerving enthusiasm into the operation and greeted every success of the darts team with the same air-punching excitement he demonstrated when Manchester United later won the European Champions League. He even continued an interest in the trade after he had started to make waves as a manager.

However, nothing was ever going to replace football, and, thanks to Ally MacLeod, Fergie was soon on the road to managerial glory, although the first streets he encountered were paved with uneven cobbled stones rather than gold. East Stirling was the first club to take a chance on Ferguson, but it could so easily have been Queens Park. This would have been a writer's dream, of course, since that was where his senior playing career had started. But when the club interviewed

Fergie, both sides were understandably nervous and nothing came of it.

When MacLeod talked to East Stirling director Bob Shaw, though, it was a different story. The Ayr manager spoke generously about the potential of Ferguson as a manager, even though he also hoped that he might still enlist him as a player–coach himself. Bob Shaw was impressed. 'Everything Ally said made sense,' he said. 'I knew Ally was an honest man and not simply trying to do a pal a favour. We were well aware of the reputation of Alex Ferguson, that he was not slow in voicing his opinions and had an aggressive streak, but if anything, that made him all the more appealing.

'You need a manager to be the boss, not just one of the lads. Work with the players, share a joke with the players, but be the boss. When we met informally at a hotel, I listened to Fergie's ambitions and opinions, and, even though there had been many applicants for the job at Muirhead, I just knew that he was by far the best man to be the new manager of East Stirling.'

The deal may have looked less favourable to Ferguson. It was a part-time job with a salary of £40 per week, and the club had a very small playing staff with only £2,000 to spend on new talent. Even in 1974 that was a meagre amount and anyone appointed as manager would have to bring their own magic wand in order to squeeze full-time thinking and planning into a part-time operation. Fergie has since admitted that he did not rush into accepting the position but gave it very careful consideration.

Perhaps it was the size of the task or perhaps it was the lack of other offers, but Ferguson eventually agreed to take on the challenge. For the first time ever, he was unveiled to the media as a football manager. 'It was quite a task,' he revealed with a smile when discussing his career in an interview some years later. 'Just three weeks before the start of the 1974–75 season, I only had about a dozen players available, none of them a goalkeeper. There was nothing much to spend and nothing much to offer anyone coming to us on a free. I had a big job on my hands, and I knew it.'

His priority was to find a goalkeeper – almost any goalkeeper! He landed an overweight and unfit Tom Gourlay from Partick Thistle reserves on a free transfer that was like most free transfers: not entirely free. The goalie's safe hands clutched £750 after signing on the dotted line, making a sizeable hole in the £2,000 transfer kitty.

The next target was Billy Hulston, a former East Stirling player who was keen to return and would be well received by the fans. The opinion of supporters has always been a consideration during football business negotiations but even more so now with so much merchandise revenue resting on the popularity of individual players. Although the re-signing of Hulston would not have led to any replica shirts being sold, his return to the club would have perhaps encouraged a few more punters through the turnstiles. Footballing ability came first, of course, but more fans on the terraces meant more money to invest in the side.

Fergie was now going through a steep learning curve as a fledgling manager. He was having to negotiate with players and with directors as well as keep the supporters happy, motivate his team and outwit the opposition. Add to that extensive travelling to watch potential players and opponents and you begin to realise the volume of new tasks that he had to get to grips with.

Anyone who thinks that players and referees are under pressure to perform should spend a day with a manager. Fergie had already gained some insight into the demands and stresses of the job by working closely with managers during his latter playing days, but nothing really prepares you for the day when it is your backside on the hot seat and you have to struggle to keep your head off the chopping block.

Ferguson's strength of character saw him through the difficulties. He has always had a wonderful ability to find alternative reasons for things not working out – such as the famous statement about the shirts being the wrong colour after Manchester United suffered a surprise defeat at Southampton a few years ago. He does not shirk shouldering blame, but, rather than allow any self-doubt to creep in, he has always managed to find other reasons for problems or failures.

Bringing Billy Hulston back to East Stirling perfectly illustrated the problems Fergie faced in his new role. The player was going to cost £2,000 but there was only £1,250 left in the club coffers. It was not a lot of use trying to negotiate with the player who had little say in anything other than his own salary, so Fergie had to try to persuade his own directors to extend their transfer budget a little more. Once he had secured the extra funds, he then had to persuade the player, who was stalling because Stenhousemuir were also in the frame for him. However, Fergie was determined to get his man and even took cash out of his own pocket to seal the deal. This gesture demonstrated the young manager's enthusiasm and determination to get his own way. He rarely fails to land a player he really wants.

When the 1974–75 season began, East Stirling were ready and got off to a flying start. They were encouraged, cajoled and scared into producing some very good League Cup results and secured seven victories and two draws in their first dozen league fixtures. The fans were up for it from the beginning, too. They liked what they had seen and heard since Fergie's arrival and knew that the attitude he had shown on the pitch would not be watered down for the dressing-room.

They were not wrong. Fergie knew what he wanted and was prepared to move mountains to achieve his goals. From the start, he ruled his players with an iron rod, and if things were not going well in a game, his half-time 'discussions' could be fierce. He might not be kicking anything on the pitch any more, but his voice could kick a backside from 100 paces.

The directors also received their fair share of Fergie's disapproval. On one occasion, the board queried the expense of bringing in a junior team to play against his own youngsters. Ferguson took the money out of his own pocket and furiously threw it at the directors with a few choice comments. And woe betide any pressmen who did not give East Stirling a fair write-up. Even though he hated it, Ferguson was prepared for criticism from respected peers, or indeed the fans, as he knew they were paying for the privilege of watching his team, but he would not stand for the opinions of lesser footballing mortals. That is one of the reasons why he fell out with the BBC on more than one occasion. When Alan Green called Roy Keane a 'lout', Fergie was furious and boycotted interviews by the BBC. Later, he took exception to a feature on Keane in the *Match of the Day* magazine and that publication was punished by a boycott as well.

A mini-revolution had been started at East Stirling, which was raising the eyebrows of many in the game. In particular, he had made many changes to the team's tactics and training practices. For example, Fergie had begun to bring the players in for a light workout on the morning of a match so that they could then spend the rest of the day together and be fully focused on the task in hand.

Ferguson also learned not to be predictable. He had different approaches for different players and for the team as a whole. Then as now he studied each player, not simply to discover their best playing role but also to understand their characteristics and to identify how to handle each one, how to motivate them and when to give praise or criticism to get the best reaction. This skill has been one of the major factors in his success. Fergie can instantly read a player or an opponent and has become famous for his 'psychological' mind games.

Fergie ensured that his players looked the part, demanding that they wear suits on the day of a match and conduct themselves as a team of professional sportsmen rather than a rabble of part-timers. He also attempted to gain any psychological advantage he could over his opponents. On one occasion, when his side was due to play local rivals Falkirk at the start of October 1974, he obtained the board's permission to take his team for a pre-match lunch at a hotel which he knew was a regular haunt of the Falkirk players. The two teams were sure to bump into each other at least once that lunchtime. Fergie knew exactly what he was doing; he was well versed in the habits of Falkirk and confidently strolled his players past their opposition. He also instructed the team to be relaxed and laugh a lot so that they would appear to be on top of the world before the serious business of the afternoon got under way. It was a ploy straight out of the Bill Shankly textbook and certainly wiped the smiles off the faces of the Falkirk players. A seed of doubt had been placed in their minds, and later that afternoon, Fergie's side won 2–0, the scoreline failing to do justice to the convincing nature of the victory.

Due to the good start to the season, attendances at Firs Park improved dramatically and there was a real buzz about the place, but Ferguson had his work cut out to keep the momentum going. He wanted nothing less than to revolutionise the whole attitude of the club. He began a new youth initiative, realising that East Stirling was never going to be able to dabble into anything other than the shallowest stretches of the transfer river, and he involved everyone at the club in the daily affairs to strengthen loyalty. He mastered a way of making everyone feel that they were an important cog in the machine without letting anyone think they were indispensable. At the same time, he soon vented his displeasure if anyone started telling him how to handle players or tactics.

Sadly, it was all over far too quickly for East Stirling. Fergie had an informal approach from St Mirren in October 1974, and more out of politeness than interest, he went for a chat with their chairman Harold Currie to discuss becoming the manager of the team from Paisley. Currie had to be very persuasive, because Fergie was enjoying himself at Firs Park, and leaving the club could not have been further from his mind. In fact, East Stirling were faring better than St Mirren at the time, so it could be argued that a move would be a step down rather than a positive career development.

'It was a tough choice,' Fergie later admitted. 'Everyone was really playing their hearts out at Firs Park and doing all I asked of them. But somehow the opportunity to become manager of St Mirren kept pulling at me.'

He also admitted that he realised that whatever he had achieved at Firs Park, the challenge was not yet completed. Yes, he had made mistakes, but by and large things were going as he had hoped, and part of him wanted to see the job through. He could not make up his mind; he needed advice.

It was to Jock Stein that Fergie turned. Ferguson had always seen Stein as the model manager and respected his standing in the game. Sir Alex has since become a willing mentor himself and is always open to similar requests for advice. In this instance, Fergie phoned Stein and asked for his opinion. Stein told him to sit up in the stand at the Love Street home of St Mirren and then do the same at the Firs Park ground of East Stirling. Surveying all he saw before him would give him the answer to his dilemma. Fergie did just that and chose St Mirren.

Nothing was officially announced until after East Stirling's game against Alloa, but the rumours were flying, proving that the boardrooms of football clubs are as prone to leaks as the Cabinet

Room at 10 Downing Street. However, Fergie avoided any media questions on the subject. Typically, East Stirling beat Alloa 4–0, and there was delight in the dressing-room after the game. The noise stopped abruptly when Ferguson walked in and, after congratulating his players on the result, told them that it had been his last match in charge. The room remained silent for several moments until the expletives started. These were followed by handshakes, though, and Fergie admitted that he left the club with mixed feelings. In some ways, he wished he had never been offered the St Mirren job but in others he knew that he was starting a new challenge with a potentially much bigger club and that had to be a good career move.

By the time he arrived at St Mirren, Alex Ferguson had already had his fair share of ups and downs. But there is no substitute for experience, and nothing ever happened to him – good or bad – that he did not stow away to be re-examined at a later date. More than most in the game, Ferguson has always had that kind of brain – quick and retentive. His wealth of experience has increased throughout the years and nothing has been discarded or forgotten. And this store of football know-how has contributed to the legacy that he has already begun to pass on to others.

When Ferguson walked into the manager's office at Love Street in October 1974, he had only been a manager for 117 days and knew he would have to call on all his resources and experience to turn things around at a club which had known better days. Although he had stepped up a rung on the football ladder, the playing side was not in the best of shape, and the complaints of the few supporters who graced the terraces echoed around a mainly empty stadium on match days.

The low attendances were partly due to the club's geographical location. St Mirren's Love Street ground is in Paisley, which is sometimes considered to be its own town and at other times a suburb of Glasgow. The club therefore found itself in the mighty shadow of Rangers and Celtic – and still does – rarely pulling in more than 1,500 fans with at least that many travelling to Ibrox and Celtic Park on a regular basis from the area. This problem would have to be addressed if the club was to make any progress.

With the poor results on the pitch and the lack of fans in the stands, it is fair to say that St Mirren was a club more in decay than in decline, but it was not beyond repair. However, the fact that Ferguson was still only a part-time manager would not make his job any easier, and it was an impossible position for a man to whom football was everything.

Despite his part-time status, he was in charge of the entire set-up; you name it, he had to sort it. The cleaning ladies would even consult him if they wanted to change the type of cleaning fluids they were using, and there is a well-known story that he was once giving a team talk when one of the general staff put his head round the door and interrupted Fergie to ask for help to unblock one of the toilets. He was also known to help with the maintenance of the pitch quite often, especially when the weather was bad and threatening postponements. It all seems a million miles away from the comparative luxury of Old Trafford that he has become used to, but I can't help but wonder if there are moments when he would like to get his hands dirty again just for old times' sake.

His first couple of months at Love Street saw little improvement on the pitch, and the patience of the supporters, who had high expectations, was tested to the full as the team's league position actually worsened. Then, during the festive season, things suddenly began to improve. Fergie changed the team around, made Tony Fitzpatrick – at 18 – the youngest captain in Scottish football and the results started to go St Mirren's way. They finished the season in fourth place, thus securing their place in what was to be the new Division One, the second tier behind the Premier

Division. The next season, against stiffer opposition, they finished in a creditable sixth place, but it was the 1976–77 season that saw real progress made and a little bit of history created for both the club and its manager.

St Mirren won the Division One championship and in so doing, secured the first piece of silverware for Alex Ferguson the manager. Along the way, he had restored faith among the supporters, entertaining them with a style of football which was based on attacking and scoring goals. He had wisely brought through large sections of the successful youth team into the first team, and he had changed the side's tactics, moving them away from the boring and crowded midfield struggle that passed for football under previous regimes and encouraging them to use the whole width of the pitch. It was exciting stuff and a real throwback to the kind of football which the good folk of Paisley had craved for so long, a fact borne out by the bigger crowds that had started to return to Love Street.

To put Ferguson's achievement in perspective, St Mirren was still a team of part-time players and the overall organisation of the club had not changed much. What had changed, however, was the approach to football that Fergie instigated. He had attempted to introduce a full-time environment and actually found part-time jobs for his players that would enable them to have more time for daily training, rather than the usual couple of days a week.

He also made a huge effort to build a relationship between the club and the local community, spending a great deal of time with local people, fans and businesses. He regularly attended meetings and functions with the supporters' club to ensure that there was a good rapport with the fans and worked hard with the local media to encourage a feel-good factor.

Ferguson was innovative both on and off the pitch. He instigated a regular supporters' magazine, and he ambitiously led the move for new floodlights which would enable better television coverage and allow the team to take part in European campaigns. Yes, he had no doubt that St Mirren would be involved in major European cup competitions before long. This record of innovation has continued at each of the clubs he has subsequently managed. Ferguson has always been swept along by his own enthusiasm for the game.

Naturally, the rest of Scottish football, including the national media, took a keen interest in what was going on in this Love Street revolution, and rumours abounded that Ferguson would soon be on his way to a bigger and better club. He did not see it quite like that. Fergie felt that St Mirren could challenge the Old Firm and stake a regular place in Europe, and even though his name was linked with taking over the reins at Ibrox from Jock Wallace, Fergie's own agenda was clearly to take St Mirren all the way to big-club status.

The only thorns in his side were his own personality and the fact that no matter how well St Mirren were faring, they still did not attract big enough crowds for him to achieve all that he wanted (despite the improvement that had been made). As a man, Fergie still had a reputation for being abrasive. He was often in trouble with the Scottish Football Association for arguing with referees or making less than generous remarks to the media after a match. He would argue with directors and with his players, and, by his own admission, 'There were times when I wish I had thought first and spoken afterwards instead of the other way round. I sometimes spoke my mind without waiting to discover what my mind was really thinking.' Perhaps this is one lesson he has never learned. Fergie has the reputation of always speaking his mind whatever the situation.

It was inevitable that some day the club and its manager would part company – no manager lasts for ever – although everything seemed to be going well at that time. Certainly, the crowds had flocked back to St Mirren with attendances regularly several times the number when Fergie took over as manager.

During their first season in the Premier Division, the side struggled but was never in serious danger of relegation. Fergie held up his hand and admitted that not getting into the transfer market when he should have done and not changing tactics often enough were his mistakes – he never once blamed the players. And despite the disappointment of the season, St Mirren had maintained their Premier Division place and were still in the ascendancy in terms of status and quality. It therefore came as a total shock when Ferguson was sacked by the board of directors at the end of May 1978.

There was no indication that this might happen; there were no rumours that his position was fragile, and Ferguson himself knew nothing about it until he attended what he was told was an emergency board meeting. He sat amazed as he was accused of breaking his contract by virtue of misconduct, a number of very thin examples being cited, such as allowing a groundsman to drive his club car. In fact, the charges against him were so ridiculous that Fergie did not even get angry. He has since revealed that he actually thought for a while that it was all a joke and started to laugh. When he realised that it wasn't, he kept the lid on his anger for once and simply walked out in a dignified manner.

The rumour mill that had been so inactive before his dismissal was now at top speed, and the media was full of little else for many days. Depending upon whose camp you were in, Ferguson was either totally innocent or was involved in such skulduggery that the board had no option but to sack him. The truth of the matter will probably never be fully revealed, but it would appear that the sacking of Alex Ferguson had more to do with a clash of personalities than anything else. He was never one to hold back from venting his wrath, no matter who was on the receiving end, and St Mirren chairman Willie Todd, who had succeeded Harold Currie during Fergie's reign, was not one to back down either.

The affair went to a tribunal which resulted in claims and counter-claims by both sides. St Mirren won the case, and Ferguson later admitted that he should not have let it go so far, subjecting himself and others to such microscopic analysis by the media and tribunal board.

Despite the acrimonious split, Ferguson left quite a legacy behind him at Love Street. The side had begun a new era in its football history with the team more than capable of holding its own in the Premier Division. They would also go on to campaign in Europe, and the club was more financially sound and cheered on by more supporters than in the years before his arrival. Fergie's dream for St Mirren had almost been realised.

When he walked away from the club, he was seething at having been sacked, but within a very short time of the bombshell that was Fergie's sacking being dropped on Scottish football and before the tribunal had even taken place, his phone was ringing to the tune of a call from Aberdeen chairman Dick Donald, a man then much respected in the game.

Ferguson was invited to go to the Granite City for an interview with the Dons chairman, and within 48 hours, he was named as the new Aberdeen manager, taking over from Billy McNeill, who had been at the club for a year and had left to return to his beloved Celtic as their new manager.

Was there ever a more appropriate place for Alex Ferguson to find international fame than the Granite City? A scriptwriter could not have dreamed up such a fitting marriage as Fergie and football in the tough north-east of Scotland, where the windchill factor is the least of your worries. 'Gritty Fergie Heads for the Granite City!' could have been the headline, but, in truth, there was so much else going on at the time that Alex Ferguson's arrival at Pittodrie warranted little more than a passing mention in all but the local papers. Scotland was involved in the World Cup in Argentina in the summer of 1978, so Aberdeen appointing a new manager was not the most important thing on the minds of football fans north of the border.

It was a pretty big deal for the club, though. Aberdeen had been also-rans for too many years, and, like the rest of the bigger Scottish clubs, they resented the fact that the Old Firm seemed to have exclusive rights to the bulk of the silverware. The Dons had last won the championship 23 years before Fergie arrived. Since then they had won the Scottish Cup and the Scottish League Cup but that was all. By the standards of most, it was a big club which generally turned in decent performances and finished near the top of the league, but it was still among those feeding off the crumbs dropped from the Old Firm table.

Before beginning his bid to break the dominance of Rangers and Celtic, Ferguson had to appoint a reliable assistant. One of the many things he had learned during the early stages of his management career was the need for an ally, something that has continued to be important to him throughout his years as a manager and a piece of advice that he has passed on to his many disciples. He may have had heated arguments with his chosen allies at times during his career, but he has still preferred to have a reliable right-hand man than go without.

When Fergie arrived at Aberdeen, Walter Smith was his first choice. Smith was playing for Dundee United at the time, although he was entering the final stages of his playing career. Ferguson knew he had a good footballing mind and felt that they could work well together. It was not to happen – for the time being, at least – because Jim McLean, Walter's boss at Tannadice, wanted him to keep playing. Instead, Fergie made former Hibernian star Pat

Stanton his second in command and set about getting the ball rolling at Pittodrie in search of better days.

Along with Stanton, there was another man behind the scenes who would do much to aid Ferguson during his time in the north, Aberdeen chairman Dick Donald. Ferguson himself has given full acknowledgement to Donald for the part he played in his further education as a manager. Donald was a fairly relaxed character who refused to get heated if Fergie was on the warpath. Instead, he would simply smile, offer his manager a cup of tea and then suggest they just sit and discuss whatever the problem might be. It took the wind out of Fergie's sails on more than one occasion. It was the chairman who also improved his manager's negotiation skills, teaching him how to deal with player contracts.

'Dick Donald was a marvellous chairman,' Ferguson later revealed to writer Jack Webster for one of his excellent books on Aberdeen FC. 'He was a gentleman, as good as his word and was always relaxed and ready to give encouragement rather than criticise. He took the view that his manager was in charge of team affairs and did not interfere unless he was asked to do so or thought there was a real need to do so.'

If Fergie had found the perfect chairman, he still had to come to terms with the egos of some of the better-known players. It was a friendly club with a good team spirit, but there were one or two players who considered themselves to be more important than the boss and were not enthusiastic about the arrival of their new manager. They were happy to lumber from game to game and accept the adulation of the fans every time they kicked a ball straight. That was not Fergie's way. He expected hard work on and off the pitch, he expected discipline and he expected results.

That will to win is one of Ferguson's greatest strengths and something that remains with him to this day. His refusal to accept second best is probably partly due to the fact that he has never forgotten what it is like to be a fan. He knows and often reminds his players that supporters remain faithful to their club through whatever trials and tribulations, putting their hands in their pockets to show their support and remaining optimistic no matter how bad things are and no matter how fierce the weather.

Fergie has always believed that you cannot buy the kind of loyalty that the fans show, but you can reward it by turning up and working hard to entertain and to get a result. That empathy with the fans has also been reflected in the managers who once served under him as players. Bryan Robson, Gordon Strachan, Steve McClaren and Mark Hughes are among those who make a point of acknowledging the role of the fans in any success their teams enjoy. They also ensure that the supporters are well treated by their players, and Ferguson himself has never been slow to make a public apology to the fans if he feels that his team's performance has been below expectations. He does not tolerate capitulation, which is why one of the greatest assets of his various teams, and especially Manchester United, is the desire and hunger to fight to the very last peep of the final whistle. He cannot stand players who hide during a game and do not give the supporters value for money.

Luckily, there were just a few players like that at Pittodrie, and it didn't take long for Fergie to sort them out. When results started to improve, the value of the new manager's harsh words and correct thinking was obvious. Even the established Aberdeen players found themselves with less and less verbal ammunition as Fergie's way proved to be the right way. There had been a serious battle of wills during those early months, but there was only ever going to be one winner. The manager was not going to budge, and the three-man board of directors was intent on backing him.

Despite his initial problems with some of the players, Ferguson inherited quite a line-up, one which included Scotland international goalkeeper Bobby Clark and young captain Willie Miller, as well as Gordon Strachan, Joe Harper, Alex McLeish and Steve Archibald, among others. By the end of his first season at Aberdeen, a good team had begun to be moulded, but they still finished trophyless. Although the potential for future success was evident and the team had come close to winning some silverware, it was also clear that there was still work to be done.

As Willie Miller explained in an interview, that first season had been an education for Ferguson and his players: 'There is no doubt that he had a tough time. We were set in our ways, and there were those who resented him coming in and changing things. One of his problems was that he was still a young man whom many had seen as a player and some had even played against. We knew of his reputation on the pitch, and in some cases there was resentment before he even walked through the door.

'When he tried to make changes, it did not go down well with some players. I had altercations with him myself, and it all got very tense on quite a few occasions. But history reveals that he got it right, and who can argue with the way he changed things?

'He was not right about everything, and he has since admitted that he made some mistakes in the way he treated people, but he changed his approach once he realised he had made an error, so you cannot say that he was totally inflexible.

'Fergie just stuck by his guns and could roar more threateningly than most. It is a measure of his character that he could face down anyone and get what he wanted. He could be genial and a good laugh if he wanted, but when he had a bee in his bonnet about something, nothing would shift him.'

Fergie's second season at Aberdeen prompted a crisis period not unlike the one that he would face early in his career at Old Trafford some years later. Aberdeen got off to a poor start and found themselves at the wrong end of the Premier Division in the early weeks of the season. A run in the League Cup kept up the optimism, and when the Dons reached the final at Hampden, the mood was definitely upbeat. However, despite having the upper hand for most of the game against Dundee United, Aberdeen had to be content with a 0–0 draw and the prospect of a replay.

'I knew we had done everything but win the game the first time round, and even though I knew Dundee United were making many changes, I did not see fit to make any counter moves myself,' Fergie admitted in a later press interview. 'That was a big mistake, and we lost 3–0. For me, it was a disaster. I don't like being beaten at the best of times, but I knew it was my fault and that was even harder to take. I did not sleep well that night. I felt very disappointed and at a very low ebb. I learned a great deal about football management by that error.'

It was a crucial moment for Alex Ferguson; a weaker man might easily have walked away from the club and the game, but Fergie was made of sterner stuff. He was the first to arrive back at the ground to meet his players after they travelled home from Dundee and greeted them almost as if they had won the cup. It was his way of owning up to his error and proclaiming a fresh start. It proved to be a masterly touch, because it showed the players that he not only shouldered the blame but felt the same disappointment as they did. He was still the boss and they knew it, but he had shown a certain human side to his personality that they had rarely seen before.

The disappointment of the League Cup defeat was soon cast aside, along with the disappointment of an exit from the first round of the UEFA Cup, and full concentration was given to the Premier League campaign which had improved after its faltering start. Although the team exited the Scottish Cup at the semi-final stage, league results were getting better.

As is often the case, the league went down to the very last

Saturday. Celtic had looked to be in an unassailable position at one point, but Aberdeen kept on winning and taking maximum points from the games they had in hand. Two victories over Celtic changed things dramatically, and when the final day of the season arrived, Aberdeen would take the title but for a major slip-up away to Hibernian. Rivals Celtic had to lose to St Mirren, but Fergie could do nothing about that. He simply had to make sure the Dons won their own game.

They won in style, a 5–0 away win virtually confirming them as champions, but the Celtic game started a little later and everyone connected with Aberdeen had to hold their breath for a few minutes until a signal from the press box at Easter Road revealed that Celtic had been held to a 0–0 draw and that Alex Ferguson's men were champions of Scotland.

There were many hangovers the next day but those suffering considered it worthwhile. Someone had at last knocked the Old Firm off their pedestal, and Aberdeen were again a force to be reckoned with. To cap the season, Gordon Strachan was named Scottish Football Writers' Association Player of the Year and was also whisked into the Scotland team for the first time. Life was very sweet at Pittodrie.

As has been seen in the Premiership in England, a number of clubs have won the championship just once and then struggled afterwards to make the same sort of impact again. That was not the case with Aberdeen. Winning became a habit that the club and its supporters found they could get used to.

At the end of the following 1980–81 campaign, Aberdeen finished with one more point than in their title-winning season but had to be content with second place, Celtic restoring their position as champions. There were other fish to fry, though, and Alex Ferguson was in charge of Aberdeen for one of the biggest games of his career so far – against Liverpool in the European Cup.

The Dons had beaten Austria Vienna in the first round and were elated to find themselves pitted against Bob Paisley's Liverpool, the best team in Europe at that time. The first leg was at Pittodrie in front of a sell-out crowd, and the Dons put up a good fight before going down by a single goal. Unfortunately for Ferguson and Aberdeen, there were players missing through injury when the two teams met at Anfield for the second leg, and Liverpool won 4–0. The Kop sang and Aberdeen faded into the night for the long journey home. Beforehand, most people had successfully predicted that Aberdeen would not be too much of an obstacle, and Liverpool continued to prove themselves superior to anyone else in Europe by going on to win the trophy for the third time.

Fergie did not use the missing players as an excuse, instead acknowledging that his team had been beaten by a superior side. He also realised that lessons had to be learned from the experience, lessons that would one day prove to be useful as he led Manchester United to European glory. That Liverpool team demonstrated to Fergie the standard that was required to be the best on the Continent.

Apart from the fairly low-key Dryborough Cup, a competition designed as a curtain-raiser to the season for invited clubs, Aberdeen won nothing in the 1980–81 season. Injuries and personnel changes contributed to the team's lack of success, and the year was described as being a period of transition. It had not been such a bad season, though, just a little bit of an anticlimax after the previous campaign. At the end of the 1981–82 season, there was further disappointment as the Dons once again finished runners-up, ironically with five more points than when they won the title. However, there was still a feel-good factor around the club with Willie Miller enhancing his legendary status by playing his 500th game for the Dons and another cup final to look forward to.

Aberdeen had secured a place in the Scottish Cup final against Rangers at Hampden Park. Ferguson prepared his side by taking them to Cruden Bay, a local beauty spot about 23 miles north of Aberdeen. When the tide is out, the beach is as flat and as smooth as the Hampden pitch, and it is one of those places with comparatively few visitors, which the media would be hard pushed to find. If Fergie's plan was to get his players away from it all, he could not have chosen a better place.

The final provided Ferguson with the opportunity to show that his Aberdeen side could not only live with but beat either of the Old Firm sides when it came to the big occasion and that the Dons' recent success was not a flash in the pan. Not that Rangers would have been likely to underestimate their opponents, especially as they knew that the Dons had beaten Celtic on the way to the final.

As it happened, the match went to extra time because of a 1–1 scoreline after 90 minutes. Fergie rallied his troops, and they seemed to be walking on air during the extra period compared with John Greig's Rangers, whose confidence had been shattered by Aberdeen's supremacy throughout the first 90 minutes. The final score was 4–1 and did not flatter Aberdeen in the slightest bit. Fergie was ecstatic but then so was everyone else wearing red.

Having won the cup, Aberdeen qualified for the 1982–83 European Cup-Winners' Cup, which was considered to be second in status to the European Cup at that time. It meant a new challenge, Ferguson's team having only participated in the UEFA Cup and European Cup previously, and he knew that his side would once again be pitted against some of the biggest names in the business.

A preliminary-round tie against Swiss side Sion was first up. Fergie decided to set the mood for the rest of the campaign and sent his players out to play as if they were up against Real Madrid. He took nothing for granted, and his players were expected to perform as if their lives depended on victory. The dressing-room after the game would not have been a pleasant place to be if they had slipped up against the Swiss team, but there was no chance of that, Aberdeen securing an 11–1 aggregate win, which included a 7–0 home victory.

Dinamo Tirana of Albania and Lech Poznan of Poland were dispatched in the next two rounds without too many nervous moments, and, suddenly, Aberdeen were at the quarter-final stage. They were drawn to play Bayern Munich, who would provide the Dons with their biggest test since they were well beaten by Liverpool in the European Cup. After the first leg in Germany, the Aberdeen contingent returned disappointed, despite having drawn the match. They knew they could and should have put the ball in the net and had let Bayern Munich off the hook. The German side were not expected to give them a second chance.

In the return leg, Aberdeen found themselves on the retreat after just ten minutes when Augenthaler put the ball in the net. It was a good goal, but there had been help from the Aberdeen defence, and Fergie was fuming. He relaxed a little just before half-time when the Dons equalised with a goal that was straight out of his own book, Neil Simpson forcing the ball over the line from close range. But when Pflugler put Bayern ahead again in the second half, all looked lost. Surely the Dons could not recover? Fergie's management skills were really needed, and he decided to make some changes. By switching a few players and putting on a couple of substitutes, including the highly talented John Hewitt, Fergie introduced a more attacking formation – and attack they did.

An emphasis on attack has been one of the key elements of Fergie's football philosophy. It has worked time after time, and his disciples have often followed his example. Steve McClaren, in particular, could never be accused of preaching defensive football.

Bayern must have wondered what had hit them. One minute they were coasting, and the next minute they were under siege. A well-worked free-kick led to Alex McLeish heading home an equaliser which brought Pittodrie to its feet, and there was no time to sit down before the rejuvenated Dons went ahead through a John Hewitt goal. There was no way back for Bayern and Aberdeen closed out the match. They then faced a much easier semi-final tie against Waterschei, a Belgian side who were overcome 5–1 and 1–0. Aberdeen had reached their very first European final.

It was, of course, the talk of the Granite City, and Alex Ferguson went from enjoying some local fame to all-out adulation. He could barely walk along Union Street in Aberdeen without stopping every few paces to shake hands with someone. Win or lose, it was agreed that Alex Ferguson had done more to put the city on the map than the entire tourism department ever had.

The icing on the cake was the fact that Aberdeen's opponents were to be Real Madrid, the team with the best pedigree in Europe. The venue was Gothenburg, and it could not have been a better choice for the Dons as the players were far more used to its northern European climate than the sun-soaked Spaniards. This advantage became even more significant when there was heavy rain before the match and the pitch was soaked.

An incredible army of 14,000 fans left the Granite City to cheer on their team and be there to witness a little slice of Aberdeen history, whatever the result. They created a great atmosphere, despite the atrocious weather, and had much to cheer when Eric Black opened the scoring after a mêlée in the box. The fans began to dream. However, a short while later, a defensive error left goalkeeper Jim Leighton with little option but to bring down the lively Santillana and concede a penalty, which Real converted, bringing them back to level terms. In those days, there was no automatic sending off, which was just as well because Jim Leighton was too good to lose.

When the final whistle blew, the scoreline was still 1–1. Fergie gave his men a pep talk before the extra period began, convincing them that the game was as good as won because Real were exhausted. That was not strictly true, but Real Madrid did seem a little slower as extra time wore on, and the clinging pitch appeared to be less of a problem for the superfit Aberdeen players. The Spanish side were stubborn, though, and kept absorbing the Aberdeen pressure and coming back for more. A penalty shoot-out seemed inevitable until sub John Hewitt, who had replaced the injured Eric Black but had not been playing particularly well, became the hero of the night. Mark McGhee planted an excellent cross into the box and Hewitt, running into the area, met the ball perfectly with his head, firing it into the net beyond the helpless Madrid keeper. Once again, the Aberdeen army of supporters erupted and kept up the noise for the remaining six or seven minutes. Real tried to find an equaliser, but the Dons dug in, and when at last the final whistle sounded, the noise was beyond belief. Aberdeen had won the European Cup-Winners' Cup, and Alex Ferguson's name echoed around Europe.

Just ten days later, the Scottish Cup was won as well, with a 1–0 victory over Rangers. It had been an amazing season once again, despite the fact that they had finished third in the league.

The 1983–84 season provided more proof that the Aberdeen renaissance was no fluke. Further European glory was denied the side when Porto proved to be too strong in the semi-final of the European Cup-Winners' Cup, although there was the European Super Cup to parade after the Dons beat Hamburg 2–0 in the annual showdown, and the Scottish Cup was won for the third time in as many seasons, this time Celtic being the beaten finalists. The championship was also won again, this time with a tally of 57 points and a mere four defeats throughout the campaign. This was the first time any club other than the big two from Glasgow had won both the league and cup in one season.

The 1984–85 season saw the fans hoping for even greater glory in Europe as the Dons tried their hand at the European Cup once again, but this time they fell at the first hurdle. It was not their year for cups, but they did retain the championship with a tally of 59 points, a new record.

Fergie wanted to do better in Europe, and the 1985–86 season certainly saw an improvement as Aberdeen battled to reach the last eight of the European Cup, only losing to Gothenburg on the away goals rule after two drawn games. The Scottish League Cup was won for the first time and in some style, the Dons not conceding a single goal in the six matches it took to gain their victory. The Scottish Cup was also won but they came fourth in the league. It was almost a bad season by the standards that they had set themselves since Alex Ferguson had become boss.

For some time there had been rumours linking Ferguson with other clubs. Rangers made an approach after the 1983 cup final, but his loyal friendship with the Ibrox manager John Greig meant that he turned down the chance as quickly as it had been offered, Fergie not wanting to offend a Scottish footballing legend. Wolves, Sheffield United and Tottenham were among the other clubs who made no secret of their interest.

At the end of the 1985–86 season, Fergie himself admitted that he was ready for a change. Whether he felt that he had done as much as he could with Aberdeen or whether it was just the gypsy in his soul, only he really knows, but he spoke to the chairman and stated his case. Dick Donald, in true form, told his manager that he understood his position but that there was no point in him leaving just for the sake of it. He should stay on at least until a suitable challenge with another major club was presented to him.

He showed great foresight, because he was very well aware that Manchester United were among the teams keen on Ferguson replacing their current manager. However, at that stage, there was only speculation and rumour, and Ferguson was still the manager of Aberdeen when the players departed for their holidays.

3

FERGIE AND THE OLD FIRM

BEFORE JOINING RANGERS AS A PLAYER, FERGUSON WAS OFTEN ACCUSED OF TRYING harder when he played against the Old Firm. He put the Glasgow giants to the sword on more than one occasion, something that continued into his managerial career in Scotland, particularly with Aberdeen when his side challenged the dominance of both Rangers and Celtic. It is somewhat ironic, therefore, that his influence has been so strongly felt at both these clubs in recent years. Why? Because Gordon Strachan and Alex McLeish, two of Ferguson's finest ex-players from the Aberdeen days, have managed Celtic and Rangers respectively. They both worked for the man, learned his wiles and his ways and have now put them into practice as managers in their own right.

During the 2005–06 season, Strachan savoured the moment as his Celtic team took the title at a canter, while McLeish had a more difficult time of it, finding himself under threat of the sack for many months and eventually being told that he would be leaving at the end of the campaign. However, he still managed to take

Rangers further in the Champions League than they had ever been before and certainly further than any Scottish club had ventured since the competition grew into its present format, and in 2005, a dramatic finish to the 2004–05 season had seen McLeish's men take the Scottish title on the final day, so it is now honours even for Fergie's former men.

Despite winning the league, Strachan's first year with Celtic was not all plain sailing, the new Hoops manager experiencing both the depths of despair and the sweet smell of success. The low point came before the Scottish season proper had even begun, his side losing 5–0 to Slovakian champions Artmedia Bratislava in a Champions League qualifier. The following week, Celtic could only muster a 4–4 draw with Motherwell, and the boo-boys began to call for his sacking. The man from Edinburgh was not about to let the criticism get to him, though, and went on to guide his team to the league title six matches before the end of the season.

It was not the first time Strachan had faced difficult times in his managerial career and had been able to turn things around. He had been involved in a number of relegation battles at both Coventry and Southampton, the two teams he had managed previously, and had kept them both up against all the odds on a number of occasions. His Coventry side were eventually relegated from the Premiership during his tenure, but the fact that they had stayed up for so long with the limited resources at his disposal indicated that he was a canny operator.

His ability to overcome the low points and turn things around are testament to his strength of character and will to win, two qualities that may not have been inherited from Ferguson but were certainly influenced and honed by him. Strachan's career has been interwoven with Alex Ferguson's, and while he might not always have found that comfortable, there is little denying that the current Celtic manager has benefited from the experience.

Strachs and Fergie first worked together at Aberdeen, although Strachan didn't begin his football career with the Dons. As an excellent schoolboy player, Gordon Strachan had been given a chance to learn his football trade with Dundee. Along with a group of other young wannabes, he commuted daily from Edinburgh where he lived with his parents, and bit by bit he matured from a schoolboy maybe into a serious teenage prospect. He made his first-team debut while he was still only 16, and during the next couple of years he was in and out of the squad until his talent made it difficult for the manager to exclude him. It was not just his ability but his outgoing character which shone through. There is a famous story that he once saw Alan Ball wear white boots and decided to do the same so that he would be better noticed by the media and football scouts. This was one thing Strachan had in common with Alex Ferguson at the same point in their careers: neither of them liked to be ignored.

As the summer of 1977 turned into autumn, Strachan was a 20-year-old recently married man who felt that he needed to widen his horizons beyond Dundee. He had proved to be a lively young player who could take on defenders, pass well and score goals. His spirit and humour were infectious, and he was extremely popular with his teammates. His energetic approach to the game was much admired, and when word went round that wee Gordon was ready for a move, there were several clubs, from both sides of the border, interested.

Arsenal were among the English sides who wanted his signature. They had seen him in action in a friendly and were impressed. Celtic also expressed an interest, but it was to their former skipper Billy McNeill that Strachan was finally sold. McNeill had become manager of Aberdeen and could offer £50,000 plus Jim Shirra in exchange. Tommy Gemmell, the former Celtic hero, was manager at Dundee and did not like the idea of losing Strachan, but the club needed cash in a hurry. The deal was soon done, and Gordon Strachan packed his bags for Pittodrie.

It must stir the emotions of managers who were themselves major players when they see how much money is being paid to professional footballers these days even before they have proved their real worth. Gordon Strachan is handling players pulling in tens of thousands of pounds a week at Celtic, and even at Coventry and Southampton some of his players were probably earning more than him. They were certainly earning far more than he earned when he first joined Aberdeen. Strachan's weekly wage was less than £100 when he moved to the Dons in 1977, but he was still considered to be on reasonable money when compared with the national average. However, today's young footballers carry more in loose change than Strachan's £85 per week.

When Strachan signed for Aberdeen, it was a time of change at Pittodrie. The promising start to a revolution during Ally MacLeod's reign as manager looked as if it might falter when he left to become Scotland manager, but Billy McNeill had taken over and things had started to happen again. However, Strachan got off to a slow start with his new club, mostly because of a bad ankle injury, and the supporters were not slow to air their disappointment at his lack of progress. Having recovered from the injury, he then found it difficult to secure a place in the first team, and there were times when he and his wife Lesley wondered what exactly they were doing in Aberdeen. The first team was going well but Strachan was not a part of it and that was painful as well as frustrating.

Strachan's first season at Pittodrie ended as it had begun. He was rarely in the first team, and if a decent offer had come in, he might have left. However, it is rare for offers to come in for players who are not being seen to perform, so there was little else to do but stick it out and hope that the 1978–79 season might be better.

A dramatic move at the end of May did indeed change matters. Billy McNeill was offered the one job he could not refuse and left Pittodrie to rejoin Celtic as their new boss. Strachan had no idea who would take over at Aberdeen or whether a new manager would bring good news or continue his misery. However, the arrival of Alex Ferguson proved to be a blessing. Although Strachan's record at Pittodrie was less than impressive, Fergie saw that the young player had real talent and realised that with some extra attention would prove to be a winner.

'He didn't say a lot at first,' recalled Strachan when I interviewed him some time later. 'He would have a laugh and chat a bit but not much. You felt as if you were waiting for something to happen, but for the first weeks, we just seemed to go through the usual routines without much changing. He was obviously weighing everything and everybody up before putting his own brand on it. Some of the older players had been worrying about the arrival of the new manager, but it seemed as if they had been worrying for nothing. There were no major changes, and, if anything, Fergie seemed to be taking a bit of a back seat.'

The young player took note of the fact that Ferguson did not rush in with all guns blazing and instead studied the situation before making any sweeping changes. It was a valuable lesson and one which would be put into good practice many years later when Strachan inherited Martin O'Neill's ageing Celtic side. He took his time before really stamping his authority on the team, and by the end of the season only Neil Lennon, Stiliyan Petrov, John Hartson and Bobo Balde remained as regular picks from the O'Neill era.

Fergie's assessment period at Aberdeen did not last for ever, of course, and it was not long before he was making his mark. 'One day he just seemed to change,' Strachan recalled. 'It was as if he had seen enough and it was time for action. His verbal lashings became frightening. Sometimes it was if he was just testing your mettle, to see if you could take it. Sometimes he seemed genuinely angry, while at other times he seemed to be acting the part. I have even seen him turn away after giving a player a real roasting and then smile at someone else in the room as if he had just turned it all on for the benefit of that one player.'

Come the new season, Strachan was a regular first-team player but that meant that he was also the focus of Fergie's fury at times: 'We used to sit there scared to move while he ranted and kicked the tea cups all over the place. Looking back now it is quite comical, but at the time you were not sure whether to say anything or just keep an eye on the teacups and be ready to duck.'

Strachan has not been dubbed 'fiery' for nothing, and it is a wonder that he and Ferguson did not come to blows all those years ago. There were occasional heated exchanges, of course, but these were usually confined to when the boss was on the bench and the player on the pitch. Strachan is known to be one of the cheeriest guys in football with an undeniable sense of humour, but he also has the reputation of being volatile at times. Although nobody has ever accused Strachan of kicking tea cups, there is every possibility that he learned the best timing for demonstrations of anger from his former boss.

He also learned about player psychology: 'Fergie used to try to fire us up before a match by telling us that the press only came to see us because they were sent by their bosses, not because they wanted to. He used to tell us that it was up to us to prove them wrong and make them want to watch us again and again. He almost told us that we were persecuted for being in the north-east of Scotland; since most journalists were based in the cities of Edinburgh and Glasgow, they looked down their noses at us.

'He also used to tell us to contest everything when we played against Rangers or Celtic, because the referees would favour those sides and be under pressure from their fans. If we contested everything, it would balance up the pressure. It was quite a ploy by the boss, because we would be looking for his words to be confirmed, and the first time a referee gave a dodgy decision against us, we remembered what he had said and it fired us up even more to prove ourselves and not let anyone put us under pressure.'

Strachan has had ample opportunity to use such ploys himself during his later spells as boss of unfashionable Coventry and south-coast castaways Southampton: 'I think you use every trick in the book to fire up your players, and, even without thinking where it came from, you use tactics that you have seen working in the past with others. There is no doubt that I learned from Alex, just as you learn from any manager.'

Having made the first team, Strachan stayed there and was a crucial part of the Aberdeen side which won the European Cup-Winners' Cup in 1983. But the relationship between himself and Ferguson gradually worsened. At the same time, Strachan became bored with the Scottish Premier League. Teams were now playing each other at least four times a season, and the challenge seemed to be evaporating for him. There were several British and foreign clubs interested in his signature, but it was to Manchester United that he was sold in the summer of 1984.

Absence is supposed to make the heart grow fonder, and when Ferguson took Scotland to the 1986 World Cup, he did not conceal his pleasure at having the talented Gordon Strachan in his squad. Ferguson was able to use that talent to mould his attacking force, and Strachan was able to see his old boss in action once again, this time at a different level. Although it was one of Scotland's worst World Cups in terms of results, the side did not play badly, and Strachan had the honour of scoring the team's only goal. At the end of the tournament and after another farewell handshake, Ferguson returned to Aberdeen and Strachan to Manchester. Neither man knew that they would meet again within a few months with Strachan once again turning up for work with Fergie as his boss.

When Strachan heard that Ferguson was to be the new Manchester United manager, he joked with his teammates that he would leave immediately and that Ferguson was haunting him. Beneath the humour there was a real concern that because the two men had not always seen eye to eye at Pittodrie, life at Old Trafford could soon become decidedly uncomfortable. But Strachan had kept in touch with his former boss after moving to Manchester and had been among the first to let Ferguson know that his name was being linked with the manager's job at Manchester United, even before Ron Atkinson had departed. And when Ferguson wanted to know about the players and squad that he was inheriting at Old Trafford, he asked Strachan, who advised him that discipline was poor and that training was more of a trot than a gallop. He also told Fergie that there was a drinking culture at the club which was not helping the team return to the habit of winning championships.

With the help of Strachan's insider information, Fergie quickly set about putting things straight. 'He knew there were problems, and he waded in to sort them without delay,' said Strachan. 'But aside from that he watched and waited for his moment and then put his own stamp on the way things were done. Some of the players did not like the changes. They had enjoyed life under Ron Atkinson. It had been much more relaxed, and even though we had not won the title that everyone wanted, we were in there challenging and picking up cups along the way.

'Fergie's approach came as a culture shock, but sometimes that is needed. Many managers make big changes just to let the players and everyone else know they have arrived and they are now in charge.'

It did not take long before Strachan and Ferguson started to have the occasional verbal skirmish. Strachan knew Fergie's methods of man management only too well and was inclined to add a few words of his own to their 'discussions'. Although it took a couple of years for them to finally part company, the relationship grew progressively uneasy, and it was probably a relief to both men when Strachan left for Leeds United in March 1989.

Strachan was a different man when he left. He was named the Football Writers' Association Footballer of the Year in 1991, a testimony to the resurgence in his career after he moved to Elland Road. He must have enjoyed every minute of his success there because the general feeling at Old Trafford before he left seemed to be that Strachan could not hack top-flight football anymore. Not only did he have a new lease of life with Leeds but he also returned to both play for and even captain the Scottish national team, an honour that might never have come his way if he had simply slipped into reserve-team football at Old Trafford. He also received an OBE early in 1993 for his outstanding services to football.

Of course, Strachan leaving Manchester United did not signal the end of his relationship with Ferguson. The years were beginning to catch up with the Leeds player after his triumphs at Elland Road, and his first-team appearances were becoming rarer when his former Old Trafford boss Ron Atkinson stepped in and offered him a place as player–coach at Coventry. Strachan had taken his various coaching badges in Scotland, and it was the perfect job for him.

'The little fellow had it all,' said Ron. 'He could still play when needed, but he had loads of experience, he had the coaching skills and something that you cannot buy – a huge heart. His enthusiasm for the game has always been the same since he was a kid, and I knew he was just the man to have alongside me when I took over at Coventry.'

It was generally thought that Big Ron would eventually move into the role of director of football with Strachan becoming team manager. A similar arrangement had worked in the past at Highfield Road, but the first quest was to avoid relegation, and as Strachan took charge on the training pitch for the end of the 1994–95 season, Atkinson remained the executive boss. Strachan shouted and Atkinson appeased.

Relegation was duly avoided, and there was optimism for the 1995–96 season. Unfortunately, Coventry once again found themselves battling for survival in the top division but somehow managed to stay up. When the next season started to go the same way, Atkinson did become director of football, and Strachan took his place as manager. Now he had to prove that he could do the job as well as everyone hoped. He was still the same Gordon Strachan – still ready to laugh, still working harder than anyone else in training – but now found himself bawling out players and yelling at officials. He had become a slightly milder version of Alex Ferguson.

It is never easy for a new manager to overcome the inevitable comparisons with his predecessor, but Strachan had an advantage. He had been there with the previous manager and had always had his own thoughts on how things could be enhanced. He set about making the club his own, and during the next couple of seasons, Coventry improved dramatically and became a mid-table side rather than constantly swimming against the relegation tide. It was encouraging, and the long-suffering fans enjoyed the upturn in their team's fortunes and were optimistic that Strachan could deliver some silverware.

That is why it was such a disappointment when Coventry were

relegated in 2001. The fans had seen the battle before but were confident that the usual late effort would save the day. This time it did not work, and their patience with the manager ran out. When Coventry were relegated, Strachan was sacked. In fairness, there was little else the board could do, and Strachan was man enough to take it. He was not the first manager to be sacked by any means. After all, even Fergie had been dismissed from St Mirren before going on to achieve greater things with Aberdeen.

Strachan has the same passion for the game as Ferguson, and he was numbed by his dismissal from Coventry, but within a few weeks, he was back in business. The Saints needed a similar job done to the one Strachan had performed at Coventry. Southampton was another side which had managed to hold its head above water in the top division for many years, even though relegation had seemed inevitable on more than a few occasions. The new boss leaned heavily on his previous experience to reorganise and motivate his players. It worked, and the highlight of his three years at Southampton was to reach the FA Cup final in 2003. Arsenal were the opponents, and Strachan sent his men out with the undertaking that, win or lose, they had to have given it their best shot by the time they returned to the dressing-room. As it happened, Arsenal won 1–0, but the Saints had their moments, and it was a philosophical Gordon Strachan who was able to tell his men they could be proud of their performance despite defeat.

Behind the scenes at St Mary's there were the usual ups and downs with players, and sometimes with directors, but Strachan seemed to be enjoying life. It came as a shock, therefore, when newspapers revealed that he would be leaving Southampton at the end of the 2003–04 season. A lot of goodwill had been built up between the manager and the supporters. They did not want him to leave and hoped he might change his mind, which is why it came as even more of a shock when Strachan suddenly announced in February 2004 that he was not going to stay until the end of the season and was leaving straight away.

The pressures of football management, family problems, health concerns – you name it, the papers were full of it. Probably the most likely reasons, though, were that Strachan needed a break, that he was getting bored again and that he did not feel that there was much more he could offer Southampton. Whatever the explanation, Gordon Strachan walked away from football – well, from Southampton at least. He continued to entertain us with his views and humour on television, which revealed that he did not really want to leave behind the game that he loved.

Meanwhile, Strachan made it clear that he was becoming increasingly disappointed with the performances of the Scotland national side, and there was talk that the SFA would soon part company with Berti Vogts and appoint a new manager. Strachan was quick to stress that he did not blame Vogts for the lack of success and instead made it clear that the problem was the lack of development of the sport at a grass-roots level. However, it was widely believed that having a foreign coach had not worked and the only way forward was to appoint a Scot with passion who experienced every triumph and every failure personally – a Scot like Gordon Strachan. The media drums banged in unison demanding Strachan's name be put on the Scotland manager's office door, but there was to be another twist in the tale.

Because of his wife's serious illness, Martin O'Neill was forced to stand down as Celtic manager and Parkhead reeled. They had just lost their most successful boss since the days of Jock Stein, and a high profile and passionate coach had to be found to replace him. Gordon Strachan was top of the list, and he was soon being unveiled as the new manager.

Despite his rocky start against Artmedia Bratislava, Strachan was not about to quit. He had been there during the first few years of Fergie's stewardship of Manchester United and had seen his boss weather the storm of criticism before his side turned the corner and went on to dominate English football for a decade. It was unlikely, therefore, that a similarly driven character as Strachan would walk away after a couple of bad results. Sure enough, he stayed, and as the season wore on, things started to improve. A successful first year in charge culminated in him being named the Scottish Football Writers' Association Manager of the Year on the back of his side's title triumph.

Strachan's grit and determination are not the only characteristics that he shares with his former manager. He has an equally wry sense of humour, feeding quips to the press on a regular basis, and he also has a ruthless streak and likes to demonstrate his anger to the full. However, Strachan is less keen to acknowledge the similarities: 'I suppose there are going to be comparisons because Fergie has twice been my boss and people expect that I will simply follow his path. It is not like that, although unconsciously there are things you see which you are bound to think of when you find yourself in a similar situation and have to sort out players, opponents, officials and tactics.

'You have to be yourself, though. Football fans are no fools – they know if you are simply copying someone else. You are expected to be innovative – that's what keeps you ahead of the game.

'I have learned from all the people I have worked with, including Alex Ferguson. You pick out the best bits, translate them into your own thinking and try to find success with them.'

Others who have seen both managers in action believe that there are similarities. Ron Atkinson watched as Strachan went off the deep end at players while coaching at Coventry. 'He could really give them some earache, and I used to sometimes wonder how much of that was Gordon and how much came from Fergie,' he said. 'Difficult to say, really, because they are both fiery Scots who care about the game and take great pride in winning.'

Strachan himself believes the greatest lesson he ever learned from Alex Ferguson was a very simple one: 'I learned that I could never be like him. Alex is a one-off, unique. There will never be another like him. I sometimes find myself pacing the touchline as he does and reacting in just the same way to things. Perhaps that is because we are both Scots and we care about football, but it can be a bit scary sometimes to find yourself morphing into Alex Ferguson.'

Strachan is right: there is nobody quite like Sir Alex Ferguson. However, there is surely a part of Fergie's legacy bestowed upon Gordon Strachan, who has twice worked for him and is trying to at least emulate his old boss in one way – to bring a European trophy back to the club he manages.

European success was also a motivation for Alex McLeish during a season in which he saw his former teammate beat him to the league title. Reaching the last 16 was quite an achievement for a side that was struggling somewhat in domestic competitions and demonstrated that some of the methods that had brought Aberdeen success under Ferguson and which had been witnessed first hand by McLeish had not gone unnoticed. However, it was not quite enough for the Rangers boss to keep his job. Throughout all the press speculation and criticism from the fans, who demand nothing less than constant success, McLeish conducted himself with a dignity that more than echoed that of his mentor.

In fact, Alex McLeish and Sir Alex Ferguson have a great deal in common. Both are Glaswegians, both had fathers who worked in the Clyde shipyards, both were avid Rangers fans when younger, and both joined the Ibrox club when they grew older. The two men also shared triumphs at Aberdeen and have regularly kept in touch ever since, Ferguson fulfilling an almost fatherly role, even though there is only about 17 years between the two men. There is no doubt that the success of McLeish as Rangers manager not only followed a similar pattern to Fergie's career at both Aberdeen and Manchester United but also owes a great deal to the younger man's observation of his former boss's approach to management when McLeish was one of Ferguson's players.

Alex McLeish was born on 21 January 1959. At that time, Alex Ferguson had just celebrated his 17th birthday and had only recently been elevated to the first team of Queens Park. When McLeish reached a similar age, he played for Glasgow United, an esteemed junior side from which a number of Scotland players had emerged in the past. He trained with Hamilton Accies, was offered a trial with East Stirling that did not materialise because the car in which he was travelling broke down, and was eventually spotted by an Aberdeen scout in 1976.

'The first I heard that Aberdeen were interested in me was when I saw something mentioned in the Glasgow *Evening Times*,' said McLeish in an interview for a book about Aberdeen. 'I had no idea they knew anything about me. I waited but nothing happened, so I carried on playing for Glasgow United and was hoping for an apprenticeship with Rolls-Royce when I left school.

'We reached several cup finals at the end of the 1975–76 season and at one of those there was a delegation from Aberdeen including the then manager Ally MacLeod and a man named John McNab, who was the area scout for the Dons. I did not know it until afterwards but he had been watching me all season. A good tip for youngsters – do your best in every game no matter who you are playing or how important the match is because you never know who is watching.'

The upshot was that McLeish joined Aberdeen but continued his studies and was also loaned to Lewis United where he gained further valuable experience in preparation for his first-team debut, which eventually came in a pre-season friendly against Fraserburgh. By then, Ally MacLeod had left to become Scotland manager and Billy McNeill was the boss. His debut match was a disaster as Aberdeen's 'poor neighbours' beat the Dons 3–0, and Billy McNeill was less than happy. The manager did not berate McLeish specifically, but he was returned to the reserves until a surprise call up for the 2 January 1978 game against Dundee United at Pittodrie. 'I was called in because a couple of the regular central defenders were what you might call "indisposed",' Alex recalled. 'It was Hogmanay, after all, but they had broken the rules and were dropped, which gave me my big chance. We won 1–0, and I hoped that I would now be a first-team regular but that came later. This game teaches you the art of patience if nothing else.'

By the time the 1978–79 season was in full swing and McLeish had become a regular first-team player, Billy McNeill had moved on to manage Celtic and Alex Ferguson had been brought in. 'Alex Ferguson was the manager who had the greatest influence on me,' McLeish admitted. 'He was there when my career was just taking off, and since we worked together many years after that as player and boss, there is no doubt that he played a major part in my career.

'We all felt the rough edge of his tongue from time to time, and while us younger players accepted it in a sense, some of the older ones got annoyed and did not take too kindly to being subjected to his temper. It was amazing how he could go from being really good natured into a total fury and back again in a few moments. I have seen him turn away and grin after really blasting one of the players. It was as if he wanted to let the others know that it was all a performance and was simply to get the player motivated.

'Sometimes it was real anger, but there were many times when he also seemed to turn it on to get the right effect. He also had a way with phrases, and I often wondered if he took time out to sit and think up some of his one-liners with a view to using them when the right occasion arose. I remember one player being told off for not shooting before he was tackled. The player said that he didn't know there was an opponent near him, to which Fergie replied, "Where did you think you were, in the Sahara desert?"

'Once you got to know Alex, you knew what to expect, but sometimes you made huge mistakes, such as the time when he was having a moan after a defeat and I simply said, "Cheer up, boss." I learned from the explosion that followed not to say anything like that again.'

In a later interview about the heady days at Aberdeen, McLeish also recalled the team talks Ferguson gave before each and every match: 'He knew how to motivate each player with a quiet word of encouragement, a stern talking to or even the threat of retribution of some opposing star player adding to his reputation at our expense.

'He might have used colourful language much of the time, but that aside, he was very articulate and knew how to put his point over. If there was any failing, it was that he sometimes got the names of opponents mixed up, but we all knew who he meant, so there was never a danger of him giving us misinformation. He was very specific about each game and each opponent and very thorough in preparing us for the match. He never sent us out there without everything having been thought out to the best of his ability.'

That is something that has been echoed by so many of Fergie's former players who have become managers. Fergie never sends his side out underprepared. Mark Hughes is a prime example of someone who has learned the same art, which is one of the reasons why his Blackburn side have been so successful in matches against Manchester United. And advance preparation is also one of the most important reasons why McLeish's team travelled further in the Champions League in the 2005–06 season than any Scottish side had in the past. Before the team met Villarreal in the first round of the knockout stages, McLeish acknowledged that his side were less talented than their opponents but believed that deciding upon a game plan in advance would help to counter the imbalance. 'Let's be honest, we don't have the players who can go and attack Villarreal,' he said. 'I think what we have to do is create anxiety in them and then try to exploit it. That can be done through players sticking to a sound plan. We have done all the homework possible, and we have been thinking about our tactics since the first leg. The players are well prepared.'

This approach could have been taken straight from the Ferguson management manual, and McLeish believes that his career has been strengthened by the influence of his old boss: 'I think all the managers I played under have made a contribution but probably Alex made the biggest contribution because he was such a tremendous influence when I was at an age to be influenced.

'It was a lesson to us all to see him take a personal interest in everyone no matter who they were. He would spend time coaching the youngsters as well as trying to get the best out of his older stagers. When Archie Knox was with him, they would regularly go on the trek to Glasgow to attend the club's youth coaching schools there. I always thought that was a very encouraging gesture to those youngsters who could go home and say they had met the actual manager of Aberdeen as well as getting the benefit of some coaching from him.

'I think that taught me the need to know each player as a person rather than simply as a number on a shirt. Each individual needs to be treated in an individual manner with the right words at the right time. Some need cajoling, some need praise and some need a dressing down. Unless you know the player, you could get it horribly wrong. Fergie is a master of knowing his players.'

Ferguson's own enthusiasm and positive thinking has been noted by everyone who has come into contact with him. Alex McLeish certainly believes that it is an outstanding part of Fergie's character and something that has been passed on to those who have worked with him: 'He is naturally progressive and forward thinking. It is second nature to him. He will laugh with the best of them and get angry very quickly, but I think I have only once ever seen him look like a man beaten and that was for just a few moments when we heard that Jock Stein had died. We were all in the dressing-room, pleased at having qualified for the World Cup but holding our breath because we knew that Jock had been taken seriously ill. Fergie came in and slumped onto a chair. I don't think any of us had ever seen him like that before and probably not since. I asked him what news and he just said, "Jock's dead." He was very, very withdrawn.'

Shortly after the sad events of that evening, Alex McLeish was selected for the Scotland World Cup squad for Mexico 1986, having established himself as a regular in the national side after making his full debut in March 1980. With Alex Ferguson taking charge of the World Cup campaign following the death of Jock Stein, McLeish knew how the new international boss was going to operate: 'He was totally focused and made us the same. Even though we were in Mexico, he did not let us off the hook to enjoy ourselves very much. When Rod Stewart wanted to throw a party for us, he would not allow it. A chat over coffee was as far as he would allow because he did not want any of us doing anything foolish during the preparations or, indeed, the tournament itself.

'He was quite right, of course, although players in a situation like that do not always see that the manager is doing his job properly. I suppose I had my moments of disagreeing with him too, but it was mostly about selection. I played in the opening game against Denmark and we lost 1–0, which was really bad luck because we had played well and deserved better. I then fell ill. It was nothing sinister, a bit like flu, but it meant that I missed the next crucial game against West Germany. I felt better for our last match against Uruguay but was left out because Fergie considered that Dave Narey had played well enough in the defeat by West Germany to deserve keeping the shirt.

'Naturally, I was angry, because I felt that I should play. I did not say anything against Dave Narey, whom I rated, but suggested that perhaps a change of shape of the team could accommodate me and I wanted to be in the action. He told me in no uncertain terms what he thought of my opinion, and we did not really speak for the rest of our stay in Mexico. It was only on the journey home that we started to chat again and put the difference of opinion behind us.'

McLeish learned that you were never going to win an argument with Ferguson either on the pitch or off it. 'I hated having to sit in his office to discuss a new contract,' he said. 'You might have everything settled in your mind about what terms you wanted before you went into the meeting with him. You had made up your mind what you would find acceptable. Then came the moment when you actually sat down to talk, and before you knew it, you had signed a contract which contained all the things he wanted and was prepared to give you and precious little of the things you had made up your mind that you wanted. It taught me a great deal about how to get a great deal.'

Negotiation skills were not all that McLeish learned from his mentor. After hanging up his boots as a player and joining the managers' club at Motherwell (1994–98), Hibs (1998–2001) and then Rangers (2001–06), he also inherited Ferguson's football philosophy, favouring attack-minded teams that attempt to play good football. However, it was only with the benefit of hindsight that McLeish was able to see the advantages of Ferguson's emphasis on this style of play: 'After taking my coaching badge courses, I think I better understood the way Fergie operated our training sessions. He used to put a lot of emphasis on attack and would have us practising crossing, finding gaps and putting the ball in the net. We would work on that for what seemed like hours, and at the time, it was easy to think that we were overdoing it a bit, but having experienced the coaching course myself, I have since seen the importance of all that work. Nobody could ever accuse Sir Alex Ferguson's teams of being defensive, and we certainly played an attacking game during his years as manager of Aberdeen.'

McLeish has inherited his former boss's footballing philosophy and has always asked his teams to play attractive, flowing football if possible. Of course, playing against the likes of Inter Milan and Villarreal in the Champions League necessitates a more pragmatic approach, but, in general, McLeish's Rangers teams have attempted to play attacking football.

Despite his relative success at both Motherwell and Hibs, McLeish struggled a little when he took over at Rangers at first, just as Ferguson had done when he first went to Manchester United, the bigger clubs bringing with them bigger expectations. There were those who were quick to criticise McLeish because they wanted someone with a more glamorous image: a Ruud Gullit or a Marcello Lippi. The immediate results did little to inspire confidence, and, for a time, the Scottish media suggested that McLeish's appointment had perhaps been an error and that Rangers would have to look for someone else.

The pressure built up even more because arch-rivals Celtic were doing so well at that time. However, to their credit, the Ibrox board did not flinch. Just as Manchester United had done when the flack was flying at Fergie during the early years, Rangers dug in their heels and let the manager get on with his rebuilding job.

McLeish was able to put into practice much of what he learned from Ferguson about preparation, tactics and the individual attention to each player, and Rangers responded. Suddenly, the tide changed, and Rangers twice took the title within a couple of years. It was exciting stuff with rivalry between the two major Glasgow sides as intense as ever, adding extra spice to McLeish's mission for success.

'I did find myself drawing a lot on the experiences I had had with Fergie, and if there was anything I was not sure of, I could always pick up the phone and ask him,' he said. 'He is always very supportive of other managers, very approachable and always willing to give a suggestion or to offer a contact here and there.

'I think that if I had to sum up the benefits of being a player with Fergie as the boss, apart from winning things, you learn how to give players self-belief. It was something that he achieved with us at Aberdeen and especially when we faced Real Madrid in the European Cup-Winners' Cup final. He treated it as another game, and that inspired us to do the same. We felt that we were going to win, that it was going to be our night and it was.

'He had tremendous mental strength, as well as strength of character, and that goes out onto the pitch with his players. That is what makes him so successful and probably the best manager of our time.'

Alex McLeish the manager has without question benefited from his time spent playing under Ferguson, and Rangers have, therefore, become beneficiaries of Fergie's legacy themselves. But there could yet be another twist in the tale, because McLeish is an outside contender to take over when Fergie finally does vacate the manager's chair at Old Trafford. Although McLeish did not deliver the Scottish championship in his last season at Ibrox and it could be argued that Gordon Strachan, having helped Celtic to the title, would be the more likely candidate, even Fergie did not win the league every year and even Fergie has experienced times when the fans have asked for his head on a platter. Either way, what goes around comes around, and United could benefit from the Fergie legacy for even more generations to come through Strachan or McLeish.

4

THE PITTODRIE CONNECTION

ALEX FERGUSON STILL HAUNTS THE MANAGER'S OFFICE, THE DRESSING-ROOMS AND the boardroom at Pittodrie. He brought never-before-seen success to the Dons and raised expectations by demonstrating that nothing was impossible. Since he left the club, manager after manager has tried to recreate those heady days, but thus far, without success. He has been a hard act to follow.

But Fergie's reign at Pittodrie spawned more than just trophies. Heroes were created, even legends, and some of those players who were sent out to battle by Ferguson have become managers and coaches in their own right.

One such Aberdeen hero is Willie Miller, who rivals Fergie himself in popularity. When the Dons went through yet another post-Ferguson bad patch in 2004, the fans demanded that Miller be brought back to the club to try to stop the rot. He was appointed director of football and the rot was duly stopped.

But Miller's route to stardom in the north-east was anything but straightforward. He made his name as a formidable defender but had previously been a forward and started his football life as a goalkeeper. It was during his soccer-mad primary-school days that Miller first went in goal. He would do anything for a game, and he actually played well enough to be selected first of all for the school team and then for Glasgow Schools Select, for whom he played in goal on a trip to the United States. 'I just wanted to play football,' he revealed in an interview. 'I was one of those kids that would volunteer for things at the drop of a hat, and that was how I came to be in goal. I enjoyed it at first, but if your team is playing well and the opposition don't come near you, it can get very boring and frustrating because you want to be in the game.'

Miller then decided that he had had enough of standing between the sticks and wanted some glory at the other end of the field, so he tried his hand at centre-forward and played for Eastercraigs, where he was spotted by a man called Jimmy Carswell, who was scouting for Aberdeen. When Miller was signed by the Dons at the age of 14, nobody had any idea just how important he would become to the club.

'It was a very exciting time for me,' Miller said. 'I was just a kid who was getting the kind of chance that only comes along once in a lifetime. I couldn't believe it was happening to me. I really wanted to be a footballer and had not really seriously thought about doing anything else. But at the back of your mind, there is always that thought that if you don't make it, you are going to have to do something else, although you don't know what.

'I was like that. I had had enough of playing in goal and enjoyed the glory of scoring goals, but, to be honest, I would have just been the guy who runs on with a bucket and a sponge if it meant that I could be involved in football for a living.'

Miller certainly used his early experience as a goalkeeper to score regularly when he was a centre-forward, but he had still to find his favourite position. Aberdeen coaching stalwart Teddy

Scott spotted Miller's potential as a defender and talked him into playing centre-half in the Aberdeen reserves. 'It clicked straight away,' said Miller. 'I knew it was going to be my position from then on. It just felt right. Teddy Scott had been very important to the young players for years, and he certainly made a huge difference to my career. He had an eye for potential.

'I was not sure that Teddy knew better than me what was going to be my best position, but he had such a great reputation for knowing what he was talking about that you could not help but respect him and just try whatever he suggested.'

When Miller made his first-team debut in April 1973, it was as a substitute against Morton, and the match provided him with just the start he needed. Replacing Arthur Graham, Willie was there to take the fans' applause at the end after the Dons had won 2–1. 'You never forget your debut,' said Miller. 'I did not have a lot to do, but it was great to be in the first team and all the better for a winning start. I was in the first team most of the time after that, and when we won the Scottish League Cup, thanks to our manager Ally MacLeod, we were thrilled to bits. But then came Fergie, and we stepped up another gear.'

Miller had already played for several Aberdeen managers before Ferguson arrived and had noted their many different styles, but he recalled the early days of Alex Ferguson's reign at Aberdeen as being something of a culture shock. 'He took a bit of getting used to because he was keen to put his own mark on the club, but he used to have an annoying habit of going on about what St Mirren did in certain situations,' said Miller. 'At St Mirren we used to do this, or at St Mirren we used to do that. It can get very aggravating when you keep on hearing the same record.

'When he first walked in as manager, he found it difficult because he felt that there were a number of senior players who had made up their minds to fight against him and be uncooperative. It is true that his style took a bit of getting used to, but there was no plot to give him a hard time.

'I had my own ideas of how things should be done, and Fergie had his. We didn't always see eye to eye, but I think we found a way of compromising that avoided too many major clashes. We had our moments, though, and they were head-on collisions. They did not bother me too much because they were just for the moment and then forgotten.

'His aggressive style of man management did not worry me personally, but there were some that it upset, and I think he might have been better advised to have changed his style to suit certain players. I think he learned that lesson himself because it seemed to me he did change. It is certainly something I learned from him. When you watch a manager in action, you don't only learn the good points, you also make a note of what doesn't work very well so that you don't make the same mistakes. Fergie's brash style did work with some, though, and it was worth learning that some players needed bawling out and some simply need a quiet word of encouragement.

'That having been said, there can be no argument that he was and still is a great motivator and tactician. Even in those days, he would select players to do a specific job against specific opponents and not just reel off the same names each week no matter who you were playing.'

What Miller overlooked was that as captain he did remind Ferguson on more than one occasion to go a little easier verbally on some of the younger players, believing that too much bawling can be as discouraging and confidence crumbling as it can be motivational. Miller once found himself rounding on Fergie after the manager had given Alex McLeish a bollocking after a 2–1 home defeat by Hearts during the 1978–79 season. The argument was leaked to the local press where it grew into reports of a major bust-up between the manager and player with physical exchanges and a shoal of transfer requests. The truth was simply a sharp exchange of words as the captain stood up to his boss in defence of a younger player.

Despite Miller's willingness to stand up to his manager, Fergie has praised him as 'one of the best players to come out of Scotland' on numerous occasions. However, he nearly lost him at one stage when Sunderland were interested in signing Miller in 1981. 'I went down to Roker Park because my contract was up at Aberdeen and Sunderland had expressed interest,' said Miller. 'It has always been a big club and one of those that any player would be interested in playing for. I was disappointed when I went for talks. I was offered very good terms and would have been much better off, but I just didn't like the place. It seemed to me that it was living off the past, and I wanted a club that was looking forward and wanting to progress. I travelled back knowing that I would not be joining Sunderland and really hoping that my future was still with Aberdeen.

'It was, of course. We agreed a new contract, and I stayed and have never regretted it for one minute. Success in Europe was the highlight but there were many other great moments and the chance to see at first hand the man who would become one of the most respected managers in world football.'

It was Miller, as captain, who enjoyed the honour of lifting the European Cup-Winners' Cup in 1983. 'It was a fantastic night, and anyone who had been nursing any grievances at that time certainly forgot them for a while. Everyone was hugging and shaking hands. As well as our own players, officials and supporters, I found myself hugging and being hugged by people I had never met before and have never met since. I even found myself hugging the boss, who couldn't stop smiling.'

A few days later, Aberdeen met Rangers in the Scottish Cup

final, which was scheduled to bring down the curtain on the season, a season which had already been committed to folklore in the north-east of Scotland. 'We all wished our season could have ended in Gothenburg,' Miller recalled. 'Once the celebrations died down, we were reminded that we had yet another important match before we could start thinking about summer holidays.

'It had been a long hard season for us, but there was some consolation in that Rangers had also had quite a busy season, so both teams were pretty tired when they took to the pitch. The atmosphere was good with more than 60,000 in Hampden, but the game itself was quite scrappy and went to extra time. There was only ever going to be one goal in it, and, fortunately, it was Eric Black who headed home for us.

'The supporters were brilliant and kept us going to the end. When the final whistle went, we were victorious. We had won another cup. We celebrated, the fans celebrated, and we happily trudged back to the dressing-room. Little did we know what awaited us.

'Fergie really ranted at us. You would have thought that we had just been well beaten instead of having won. He picked out myself and Alex McLeish as having done our bit but berated the rest for being below par. We couldn't believe what we were hearing, and a lot of the players were really angry about it. It was the strangest post-match talk from a cup-winning manager I have ever heard.

'In fairness, some time later Fergie did get everyone together and apologise. He put it down to being tired himself and cutting loose without thinking properly. He was at least man enough to put it right. You have to give him credit for doing that.'

It is also possible that Fergie's explosions were not simply for effect or because he was bad-tempered; nervous tension can change a character dramatically. 'Alex used to be quite tense before a game and would fidget a lot,' Miller recalled. 'I don't know if he is still the same, but we used to notice it. I think the only time I can remember him being really relaxed was on the night of the European Cup-Winners' Cup final in Gothenburg.'

Miller joined the Aberdeen coaching staff when he came to the end of his playing career and after the departure of Alex Smith, who had succeeded Ferguson, became manager of the club in 1992. He was still held in high esteem in Aberdeen, and there was a buzz of excitement when he became the boss. In his first season in charge, Aberdeen finished as runners-up in the Premier League, Scottish Cup and Scottish League Cup. To come close to winning a Treble in his first full season as manager was pretty good going.

'I always had my own ideas on how things should be done, but there is no question that you cannot help but put into practice things you have picked up from other managers, even mistakes you have seen them make,' said Miller. 'Alex Smith was a good manager, but there is no doubt that the Fergie influence remained at the club and on individuals like myself. There was no way anyone could be like him, but his thoroughness and his approach to each game could hardly be bettered, so the wise thing was to follow a similar line.'

By 1995, Willie had kept Aberdeen close to success without actually taking a trophy, so he left the job to make way for someone else to rekindle the Fergie magic, but nobody has succeeded yet. Fergie is a hard act to follow because he creates a benchmark by which all others are judged, even though they may not have the same formula for success.

'The lack of real trophy success at Pittodrie since the Fergie days says a lot about the man,' said Miller. 'He created something great at Aberdeen, but it's a bit like being an inventor. Sometimes when you are the person who has created something, you are really the only one who truly knows how it works. I think that is true of teams created by Fergie. Other people may take them over and on paper it should all go on just the same but that special ingredient is missing. Alex himself is the missing ingredient. Without him being there, his teams do not operate so well or so smoothly for others. He can get performances out of players who simply do not play the same for others.'

Having had a reasonably successful spell as Aberdeen boss himself, Miller is now back at the club as director of football. He knows not to interfere with the manager's job but works away in the background and is able to supply advice as and when it is needed. His observations of Ferguson in the past have been of benefit in this role, and while Miller is behind the scenes, Sir Alex Ferguson's presence will continue to be felt at Pittodrie.

Having worked with him for so many years, Miller believes that he knows Ferguson well enough to have identified the two most important aspects of his former boss's personality that have contributed to his success: 'I think you can sum them up in two words – desire and belief. He was himself totally committed and focused and has obviously made great sacrifices for his career and for his clubs. He expects everyone else to be the same. If you pull on the shirt, you should be committed to winning and have a strong belief that you will. That is the Fergie way, and it is obviously a successful one.

'I think another of Fergie's great strengths is being able to quickly sum up a situation and people and have the intelligence and flexibility of mind to be able to deal with things in a way that is needed at the time. He is very good at knowing what players need and who he can rely on, both on and off the pitch.'

When Aberdeen celebrated its centenary in 2003, which also coincided with the 20th anniversary of that great night in Gothenburg, Willie Miller was one of the leading figures at the various events, as was Sir Alex, who returned to Pittodrie to speak at two major dinners. 'It was almost like turning back the clock,' said Miller, 'except that we were all that much older. Many of his former players sat around as he spoke, and by the time he had finished, I think all of us felt that we could get our boots on and go and do it all again.'

Another key figure from the Dons Cup-Winners' Cup side that attended the centenary celebrations was Mark McGhee. Although McGhee went from being very close to Ferguson to being virtually alienated by him, he still believes his managerial career has benefited from working with his former boss, and he has been strongly influenced by the Fergie legacy.

Mark McGhee was Alex Ferguson's first signing when he took over at Pittodrie. It was not the first time he had shown an interest in the player. When Fergie was manager of St Mirren, he had pursued McGhee, who had caught the eye of a number of clubs with his clever ball skills while playing for Greenock Morton. On that occasion, Fergie was thwarted, and it was Newcastle who took the plunge and signed the young and very talented Scot. There is no doubt that Mark McGhee could have stayed with Newcastle for the rest of his career, or at least have remained in English football where the rewards might have been higher, but the chance to move back to Scotland was tempting and a price tag of £70,000 was also appealing to Newcastle. McGhee signed for the Dons, and Fergie had finally got his man. McGhee would add extra width to the side's attacking play, the player equally happy to hug the touchline and stretch the opposing defence as to play straight down the middle as an out-and-out striker.

'It was an interesting time,' said Mark. 'I got the occasional ear bashing like everyone else, but it was not so bad. My job was to feed our recognised strikers, although I used to be able to cut inside fairly often and try to lay on a goal for someone else. I scored a few myself, but I made a lot of others.

'Fergie liked his players to train hard, and I had no problem with that. I enjoyed training. Fergie used to keep a hawk eye open, so woe betide anyone who might be slacking. When he talked about working hard, he did not just mean at match time.'

Ferguson greatly admired McGhee as a player and was disappointed to lose him to Hamburg after many happy years. He later commented, 'Mark McGhee had great skill and tremendous resilience. When I knew he was going to leave us, I remember talking to Willie Miller and saying how much we were going to miss him. In my opinion, he was a greater loss than Gordon Strachan or Doug Rougvie.

'John Hewitt had become a hero because of scoring big-time goals in games where it really mattered. We also had Eric Black, who was a great finisher and especially good in the air, but they were both influenced by McGhee, whose ability to beat defenders and accurately cross the ball was superb. He was a match winner.'

That proved to be true in Gothenburg when Mark McGhee played such a major part in making history as Aberdeen brought home their first European trophy.

When McGhee did leave, Ferguson admitted that he blamed himself for losing the player. After the successful Cup-Winners' Cup final, McGhee had been due for an improved contract, but Fergie haggled with him. As a consequence, a disgruntled McGhee felt that the only way he was going to progress was to move to another club and eventually moved to Hamburg for £300,000. Ferguson believes that he haggled too hard when they discussed the player's future; if he had been more flexible, McGhee might have been happier and stayed at Pittodrie. That is open to debate, though, as, ultimately, Hamburg, as champions of Europe, had more to offer than Aberdeen. While the Dons may have beaten them in the European Super Cup, Hamburg were the more glamorous club.

The move certainly added to McGhee's knowledge and

experience of the game as a player and would one day be useful when he turned to management. 'It was a valuable experience for me and one which few British players were ever able to gain because there was not as much passage of players from country to country as there is now,' he said. 'You find yourself involved in different coaching techniques, different kinds of match preparation and, in some ways, a different football culture. You can learn a lot from such a move if you are interested enough to want to. I was.'

Ferguson did not hold any grudges as a result of losing one of his star players to the German outfit, and the two men's paths crossed a number of times while McGhee was still a player. After Hamburg, McGhee joined Celtic and played against Aberdeen on several occasions. Even later, he returned to Newcastle and lined up against Manchester United after Ferguson had become boss. McGhee reminded his former manager that he still had a magic touch when he scored against United in a 1989–90 FA Cup fifth-round tie. Fergie had the last laugh with his side winning 3–2, but he was reminded that McGhee still hit the target more often than not.

Ferguson and McGhee kept in touch, and Sir Alex even put in a good word for his former player when McGhee was in the frame to become manager of Reading. It was perhaps his recommendation that swung the decision in McGhee's favour.

'I knew what I wanted to achieve as a manager,' said McGhee. 'Like a lot of people, you want the chance to prove yourself but do not necessarily get the opportunity. Reading took a gamble on me, though, and during my three and a half years at the club, things did not turn out too badly.'

With just 53 defeats in 183 competitive games, McGhee accumulated an impressive record for someone in his first senior managerial role. It was a good enough record to attract Leicester City, who made him an offer he could not refuse. Throughout this time, McGhee kept in close touch with Alex Ferguson. 'We spoke regularly,' he said, 'and he was a big influence on me, because he was always quick with advice, whether I asked for it or not. With his experience and fantastic track record, you could not help but be delighted to have him on your side.

'I did learn a lot from just seeing him in charge at Aberdeen. He did not get it all right, and he would be the first to admit that. Having said that, he got a lot more right than he got wrong, which is why Aberdeen flourished under his management.

'He had different methods to motivate different players, and you could never really argue against the way he did things, because he was usually proven to be correct. His preparation was always excellent, and he knew how to give players a lift when they needed it.

'When we were playing in Gothenburg for the European Cup-Winners' Cup, he invited Jock Stein along, and his very presence was enough to ensure that everyone played out of their skins. Fergie left nothing to chance and was always thinking one jump ahead of everyone else.

'He was always a hard man to please, but if you did please him, he let you know it. We shared some great moments when we were at Aberdeen, and since I have become a manager, he has been a good friend.'

McGhee suddenly left Leicester in December 1995 to become manager of Wolves, only a year into his tenure at Filbert Street. It is suggested that he took advice from Alex Ferguson, who thought it would be a good career move for his former player. Commentators have stated that it is possible that Fergie also thought it would be a good move for his son Darren Ferguson, who was a Wolves player at the time.

Unfortunately for McGhee, he was never really able to get the club where he wanted it during his nearly three years as manager. 'It was never going to be an easy club to manage, whether it be me or anyone else,' said McGhee. 'Because of the tradition of the club, its size and the size of the local population, there is always a great air of expectation hanging around Molineux. Wolverhampton Wanderers is a big club which is waiting to be woken from its slumber. I got part of the way, but it needed more investment than was available at the time.'

While McGhee was manager of the Midlands club, Darren Ferguson did not see much playing time, and McGhee has said that the regular phone calls and words of advice stopped some time after he took over. He is quick to point out that it might simply be that he did not achieve anything much as Wolves manager and Fergie gave up on him, but the more cynical of observers, including Michael Crick in his book *The Boss: The Many Sides of Alex Ferguson*, have suggested that Darren Ferguson's lack of real progress might also be a factor. Ferguson himself has commented that Darren's career in the game has suffered because of his family name: 'He is the best player outside of the Premier division by far. But he is hamstrung by who his father is. Managers will not touch him because of me.'

Since leaving Wolves in 1998, McGhee has further proven his managerial mettle at Millwall, another club that has been difficult to manage over the years. He took over in September 2000 and steered the London side to the Division Two title in his first season. And although he had departed before the team reached the FA Cup final in 2004, there is no doubt that he played a major part in getting them there.

From Millwall, he became manager of Brighton and Hove Albion in 2003 and endeared himself to the fans by keeping the side from relegation. However, Brighton fans are used to the ups and downs of football and would probably not have been too shocked when their team was relegated from the Championship at the end of the 2005–06 season.

Although Mark McGhee is yet to become the manager of a Premiership side, his track record shows that he has the potential to be one of our top bosses. 'I would like to be a Premiership manager one day,' he has said. 'I think if I lacked that kind of ambition, I would be in the wrong job, but who is to say that it cannot be achieved by taking a smaller club all the way to the top. It has been done before, and one of the great things I learned from Sir Alex is that nothing is impossible.

'When we were at Aberdeen, he was always hungry for success. Even when we had just won a trophy, he quickly moved on to the next one. He never stopped being ambitious to win something bigger or to win the same prize again. I think that he drove that into us so much as players that none of us could ever be any different.

'Fergie never accepted his team or his individual players as being second best. That was not good enough. He never accepted anything less than total commitment and effort, and he always wanted his teams to be attacking and exciting. He could not stand mediocrity of any sort.

'I think every manager must want 100 per cent from his players and will work hard to get it from them, but Alex has always had a way of being able to motivate that [attitude], even if it meant yelling very fiercely in someone's face.'

Although he has served under a number of managers and has gained quite a bit of management experience himself, Mark McGhee believes that Sir Alex stands head and shoulders above everyone else. 'You have to look at what he has achieved and how he has achieved it,' he said. 'He won a European trophy with Aberdeen and might well have done it again if he had not moved to Manchester United. He was rebuilding Aberdeen for a second time when he left.

'Then he moves to Manchester United and completely rebuilds

the team there, not just once but several times, making some great signings and bringing youngsters into the side at just the right time. The United trophy cabinet has never been so full. Since he went to Old Trafford, they have won the European Cup, championships, Doubles, a Treble and just about everything you can think of. That is some record. There are other excellent managers in the Premiership, but they all have a long way to go before they achieve anything like the volume of success of Fergie.'

McGhee is a fan of the Fergie style of play, which gives value for money win or lose with its emphasis on a determination never to give up, to attack and to play good, open football: 'Alex not only likes his teams to entertain, he likes to see them playing stylish, attacking football. He likes smooth passing, good technical build-up and a clear-cut finish. He likes speed and aggression, which is why United are famous for turning defence swiftly into attack, and also likes his teams to keep going right to the final whistle with as much effort put in during time added on as they put in during the first ten minutes of a game. He likes his players to be very fit and strong and to be prepared to be goal hungry in attack and tough but fair in the tackle in defence.

'Whether it is being like-minded or whether it is the Fergie influence I don't know, but I like my players to produce the same kind of football and have the same approach to each game as Sir Alex expects from his players. Defeat is not an option.'

At the Aberdeen FC reunion dinner in 2002, Mark also said that he admired the work Ferguson put into seeing players with a view to buying them for the club. 'He would travel anywhere at all in the worst of weathers to take a look at a player who might be anything like the grade that was required by the Aberdeen youth section.'

Fergie also develops a great rapport with the supporters and really endeared himself to those who went by boat to Gothenburg for that famous night. 'There were thousands of Dons fans there on the night,' McGhee recalled, 'and Fergie discovered that almost 500 had travelled by ferry and would be returning to Aberdeen on the *St Clair*. We returned ahead of them because we flew, so Fergie made a point of taking the trophy down to the docks to greet them. I went with them, and he showed them the cup as they came off the boat and shook hands with just about every one of them. It was a tremendous gesture and quite unique because usually the fans are there to greet the returning team rather than the other way about. That was Fergie's style of supporter management.'

McGhee is an intelligent man with a wealth of experience as a player and a growing pedigree as a manager, even though he is yet to make it to the very top. He has learned much from Fergie, including the essentials of match preparation. It seems only a matter of time before he lands a big job or brings success to a smaller club. He may even one day manage a team playing against his mentor's in the Premiership – the sorcerer versus the apprentice.

Another manager waiting for his big chance is Neale Cooper, who might well develop into a highly successful manager one of these days, even though he was sacked from his most recent job with Gillingham. Cooper is not a new kid on the block – he has been around as player and manager – but one thing is for certain: he learned a great deal while playing for Aberdeen under the guidance of Alex Ferguson, and his word is respected in the game.

Neale Cooper was one of Fergie's fledgling stars during his first year in charge of the Dons. As well as paying immediate attention to the needs of the first team, Fergie has always been keen to promote schemes for the future with the emphasis on establishing a continual flow of young lads from the youth set-up into the senior squad to keep up the forward momentum of his clubs. He reinvigorated the youth scheme at Manchester United, and the club now has a youth policy which not only finds and nurtures talent from Manchester but from throughout the world. At Aberdeen, he also set about creating a strong youth policy, and Neale Cooper was one of the products of that talent-spotting and propagating organisation.

Like many of the Aberdeen youngsters of the time, Cooper provided emergency cover when the first team was depleted by injuries, and it gave him a taste of the regular football that was to come. 'Pittodrie was a great place to be because there was such a buzz about the place,' Cooper recalled. 'The young lads like myself felt a part of the set-up, and when we were called into the first team because of injuries, we were treated just like senior players. There was a good atmosphere in the dressing-room and among the supporters. You felt as if you were a part of a club that was going places.'

Cooper developed as an uncompromising defender – fair but uncompromising. With Fergie inspiring him, he could be little else. He was always prepared to get in amongst the action, and that brought him a few goals, too. He could certainly strike a ball and scored more than one long-range effort that broke the hearts of opponents. He developed well in the youth set-up and rewarded his manager with performances which were rarely anything other than first class.

When Aberdeen beat Rangers 4–1 in the 1982 Scottish Cup final, it was the 18-year-old Cooper who not only played a man's game throughout but scored the fourth goal. He broke through, took the ball past the Rangers keeper Jim Stewart, rolled it to the goal line and then hit it with full force into the roof of the net as a gesture of triumph.

There were still greater things to come, of course, including the European Cup-Winners' Cup final in Gothenburg. 'It was a night to remember for ever,' said Neale. 'It was a real team effort, and there was great spirit in the dressing-room. There were four of us young lads in the squad: Neil Simpson, Eric Black, John Hewitt and me. We had grown up together at the club, but we had also become regular first-team players, so there was no separation from the older players. We were all in it together, and we felt that as we prepared for the game, as we went out on the pitch and as the game went on.

'The boss made us feel like a unit and urged us to play for each other. I think that made a big difference because we were prepared to give it everything and not think about anything other than that match on that night. We were fully focused individually and as a team. It worked, didn't it? Sometimes beating the great Real Madrid to win the European Cup-Winners' Cup still feels like a dream.'

Just before the departure of Alex Ferguson, Neale Cooper joined Aston Villa but never really settled and finally returned to play in Scotland again, ironically for Rangers, against whom he had taken such delight in scoring that cup-final goal some years earlier. From then on, whenever he played at Pittodrie, he pulled on the blue shirt of Rangers but few Dons fans could resist giving him a round of applause for the sake of 'auld lang syne'.

'Neale Cooper was a dynamic young player,' said Ferguson when celebrating the 20th anniversary of Aberdeen's European triumph. 'He quickly established himself as a first-team player and had great passion and courage. You knew he would never give in at any stage of the match, and that means a lot to a manager, because one player in your side like that can keep all the others going right to the final whistle.'

Neale Cooper has his own memories of playing for Fergie. 'Fergie was a stickler for fitness,' said Cooper. 'He felt that it was important that players could keep going from the first blast of the whistle to the last. Many Manchester United games have been won in the closing stages of the second half when opponents were tiring.

'He was always on to us about passing and keeping possession. He was right, too. If you have the ball, the opponents aren't going to be scoring any goals, so the common-sense thing to do is to keep hold of it. Good passing has always been a trademark of his teams and so has constant pressure on the opposition. Most often opposing teams are worried about committing themselves because of counter-attacks. When you can make another side feel pressured, even when it is on the attack, you know you are achieving something.'

Ferguson has always been a strict disciplinarian, and Cooper told Aberdeen football historian Jack Webster that journeys home after an away defeat were very tense. 'You felt really guilty if you lost,' he said. 'We used to laugh and joke a lot on the way to matches, because you never knew what the atmosphere was going to be like on the way back. If the boss was not happy with a result, woe betide anyone who tried to make light of it before he was ready to get positive about the next match.'

When Neale Cooper was ready to turn his hand to management, he remained in Scotland and steered Ross County from obscurity in 1996 to being a side to reckon with in 2002. His early experiences as a boss were not unlike those of Alex Ferguson when he started the road to management fame with East Stirling, a small club with big ambition but not much financial clout to help them get where they wanted to be.

Ross County remains an ambitious club knocking on the door of the Scottish Premier League today, and that is in no small part a tribute to the management skills of Neale Cooper, who went on to prove that it was no fluke when he became manager of Hartlepool in 2003. In England, he turned round Hartlepool's fortunes by taking them close to promotion from Division One to the Championship during the 2003–04 season. Although they only made it to the play-offs in the end, reaching that stage signified a complete turnaround in the club's fortunes.

A new challenge presented itself in 2005 when Neale Cooper took over the reins at Gillingham. Once again, it was a question of changing the fortunes of a club which has the local support to get behind a Premiership side but for too long has had to make do with lower-division football. There might have been no instant answers at Gillingham, and Cooper has since moved on, but he has proved during his short managerial career that he is up to any challenge and that he is well able to create an upturn in a club's fortunes.

One of the ways that Cooper has attempted to change the fortunes of the clubs that he has managed has been with the development of robust youth policies. This has been especially important because of the limited resources that have been available to him. This process closely resembles that undertaken by Ferguson, who has seen generations of players come through the ranks of his teams' youth set-ups to reach the very top of world football. Fergie has never forgotten his own early playing days and encourages his clubs to create opportunities for as many youngsters as possible. Neale Cooper has the same ethos and has preached the gospel of a strong youth policy at each of his clubs.

Despite the similar emphasis on youth football as Ferguson, Cooper thinks of himself as his own man but admits that he has applied some of the things he learned playing for his former Aberdeen boss to his own managerial career. 'I don't consciously copy anyone else,' said Neale. 'However, there is no doubt that if you see something which works, you try to make the same approach work for you. I saw plenty when I played for Sir Alex and gained a great deal to try in my own career as a manager.'

Cooper is one of those people who finds it hard to keep away from the game, and what a waste of experience and talent it would be if he does not find new challenges within football. There is no doubt that he has learned much from Fergie and perhaps needs a bigger platform on which to express himself.

Alongside Neale Cooper as he progressed through the youth system at Aberdeen was Eric Black, another local lad who made good. 'I first saw him when he was 13,' said Fergie. 'Eric fulfilled all our expectations plus some. He was a great goal scorer with excellent ball control and pace, and very good ability in the air.'

Black and Cooper both broke into the first team at Aberdeen at just about the same time. They both had a tremendous impact, and having put them in the side, it was difficult to leave them out. They might have been youthful and inexperienced when compared with some of their teammates but neither player was fazed by the big occasion. Black even scored on his European debut against all-powerful Hamburg. However, Fergie later wondered if he had asked too much too soon of his young players and used Black as an example of someone who was brilliant in his earlier career but seemed to suffer from burn-out when he should have been peaking during his late 20s.

Black was one of the fans' favourites at Aberdeen, having scored a whole string of exciting goals often at crucial moments. He looked set to be a Dons player for ever. But he was quite canny from an early age, and while many might have thought he was going to be at Pittodrie for the rest of his career, he had other ideas and left to join the French club Metz in 1986. 'Fergie had a reputation for being harsh at times, so I was not looking forward to telling him that I was going,' said Black. 'As young lads, we had seen both sides of his character. He liked to have a laugh with us and make us feel that we were as much a part of the club as anyone else, but we also knew what it was like to get a blasting from him. We grew up with that, and even though we became first-team regulars, the treatment was the same: he would praise where he felt it was warranted but give us some dreadful dressing-downs if he felt we had not given our best.

'When I told him I was going to leave to join Metz, I didn't know what he would do. I hoped he would wish me well, but I expected a blasting. I got the blasting and was dropped from the side for the last couple of games. He felt that I should have told him that I was thinking of going, but I don't know if his reaction would have been any different if I had.'

Ferguson was so annoyed at Black's departure that he even dropped him from the side to face Hearts in the 1986 Scottish Cup final and made a statement before the match in which he said, 'Eric Black will take no part in the Scottish Cup final. He has played his last game for us. I feel that it is only fair to the other players who have been loyal to the club that he should take no part on Saturday.

'It was a painful and difficult decision to make, but I feel it was the right one. The player's contract is not up until 30 June, but he has signed for Metz. Aberdeen will have nothing to do with agents for any player. Someone has to take a stand against this practice and show their displeasure with what is going on. We are big enough to do that by not playing Eric Black against Hearts on Saturday.

'It is really a sad end to Eric Black's career at Aberdeen. He has been with us since he was 13, through all our ups and downs. When he had a severe back complaint, we stuck by him. It is a great pity that it has happened this way, but his decision to deal through an agent has cost him his place on Saturday. He has now gone to an insignificant club, and his agent has done him no favours at all. It is a travesty that Eric Black, a player like him, should be going to a club like Metz.'

It was a calm statement but a telling one. Fergie was clearly unhappy about the manner of his player's move and the involvement of an agent. Since then, of course, he has dealt with many agents himself, so it was a gesture against an incoming tide.

As for Eric Black, he did go to Metz and did not appear to have any grudge against his former manager for leaving him out of the 1986 Scottish Cup final. In fact, he has since spoken well of Ferguson in various interviews. 'He was great with us young players,' he said. 'It is easy to feel ignored when you are a youngster at a club, but Fergie's approach was that young players needed special attention to encourage them and to make them feel at home.

'When you become a first-team player, even a young one, more is expected of you, and Fergie considered that if you were good enough for the first team, you were good enough for a blasting. Some people might not consider him to be among their favourites, but you have to give credit where it is due, and he has certainly made his talents work for him and for his clubs.'

Eric later became development manager at Celtic, where he took charge of many young hopefuls. He never forgot what he learned from Fergie and his approach to youth football as the nursery from which the players of tomorrow's first team will come. Fergie believes in working his youngsters hard in preparation for their careers at the top level.

'I had an enjoyable playing career, but I also learned a lot that has helped me with my coaching work,' he said. 'You learn from everyone, but what I especially learned from Fergie was discipline and the setting of high standards from an early age. Not to make it mission impossible for them but to present them with a high standard to attain. Young players are even more vulnerable these days, because they earn so much money and have so much done for them that they could easily get carried away and not bother listening to what the boss has to say. They have to learn that they must knuckle under and earn their living and their privileges.'

Eric Black left Celtic to become manager briefly at Motherwell and then Coventry before joining Birmingham to become Steve

Bruce's chief coach and right-hand man. It has to be said that while his spells in charge of Motherwell and Coventry were not long enough for him to make any serious impact, he was working without any real financial clout and perhaps a bit more time with a club with a bit more money might have seen better results for his efforts. However, he is happy enough at Birmingham with Steve Bruce and is well aware that his experience of working with Fergie will be of benefit both to him and to the team, especially as they fight to regain their place in the Premiership. 'I did learn a lot from Fergie,' said Black. 'He has a very quick mind and can switch tactics several times in a game. He is very quick to spot a problem and to know how to deal with it. He gets involved in coaching but only up to a point, because he likes to have an overall picture, and if you are too intent on the small details, you don't always see the whole picture. He knows about motivation, too, and is an expert. If you can't learn from him, who can you learn from?'

It is a sentiment with which Willie Miller, Mark McGhee and Neale Cooper, who came under the wing of the great man at the same time as Black, would agree. All four have medal collections of which they can be proud and memories they could dine out on for the rest of their lives. As well as giving their all in service to Aberdeen under Ferguson, they have developed into figures who could yet influence the British game a great deal. Those that benefit from the influence of these four men are all indirect beneficiaries of the Fergie legacy themselves. And in this way, the repercussions of Ferguson's management of Aberdeen are still being felt in the game today, despite the fact that he left the north-east so many years ago. But although Fergie's reign at Pittodrie certainly had an impact on the club and on the lives of those around him, his biggest impact was still to come.

5

FERGIE'S INTERNATIONAL LEGACY

THE LONG ARM OF FERGIE STILL REACHES OUT TO THE SCOTLAND NATIONAL SIDE decades after his brief encounter at international level. His pal Walter Smith is now in charge and among the Scotland regulars is Darren Fletcher, who pulls on the shirt of the Red Devils between internationals.

Ferguson wouldn't have become involved at all with the national set-up if it hadn't been for the influence of one man: Jock Stein. Stein is perhaps most famous for having been manager of Celtic when they became the first British club to win the European Cup back in 1967, and he is a real football legend, one of the all-time greats. It was not just the silverware he won that made him the man he was; Jock Stein was a gentleman, quiet and thoughtful, but a veritable terrier when the situation called for it. His enormous presence stemmed from a quiet dignity and genuine authority, but there was a very human side to him, too, making him similar to Sir Matt Busby, Bill Shankly and Bob Paisley.

Jock Stein was much loved and admired, especially by those

who came into direct contact with him. It did not matter who you were, how old you were or how well he knew you, he was always well mannered, and if you had met before, even briefly, you could almost guarantee he would remember your name. He took an interest in people and was a friend and mentor to many, among them Alex Ferguson.

The relationship between the two men was cemented when Ferguson was invited by Stein to become his assistant following the younger man's success at steering Aberdeen to that European Cup-Winners' Cup. Jim McLean had been Jock's assistant, but when he resigned in the summer of 1984, there was only going to be one replacement and Ferguson landed the job. In fact, Stein had been monitoring Ferguson's career for some time, and the two had often chatted while opposing managers. In this way, Fergie benefited from Stein's experience and knowledge even before he worked with him. However, the real education came when Ferguson sat beside Stein in the Scotland dug-out. 'I learned something with every match,' Ferguson once admitted. 'Jock's way of handling players and situations and even the various officials, his psychology and his general style were masterful. He was also a great raconteur, and it was a very special experience to sit listening to him talking about life and imparting his many anecdotes. He was not loud nor did he talk about himself much, just about life and, in particular, football life, of course.'

The qualifying campaign for the 1986 World Cup progressed reasonably well, leading up to an important final group game in Cardiff against Wales. A draw would see Scotland through to a two-leg play-off against Australia, the ultimate winner going to Mexico for the World Cup finals. But no one could have predicted exactly what drama would unfold on that fateful evening at Ninian Park.

On the evening of the match, Stein had not been feeling very well, and Ferguson even said as much to Gordon Strachan, who had been about to stage a one-man protest at half-time when there was a suggestion of him being substituted. During the second half, Strachan was indeed substituted and replaced by Davie Cooper, and it was the latter who scored from the penalty spot to make the score 1–1 and give the Scots the result that would see them through.

Moments before the final whistle, Stein stood up. He had mistakenly thought that the referee had blown his whistle to end the match. As he stepped forward to shake hands with Mike England, the Wales manager, he stumbled and Ferguson had to catch him. He knew that the Scotland boss had been feeling worse as the game had gone on but had no idea just how seriously ill Stein really was. While the team doctor and various other medics helped Jock away, Ferguson took charge of the players, and it was only a little later that it was announced that Jock Stein had suffered a heart attack and died.

Having become good friends with the Stein family, it was Ferguson who contacted them to give them the bad news. He then continued to go through all the post-match arrangements with the players in the dignified manner that Jock would have expected. It was only much later that he was able to relax enough for his own personal grieving. Fergie had a huge amount of respect for Stein and was honoured to have been his assistant. He learned much from the elder statesman of Scottish football but also connected with him on a personal level. He knew that the great man's loss would be deeply felt.

In the wake of Stein's death, Fergie was asked to be caretaker manager of the national side for the remainder of the World Cup campaign, which was quite an honour considering the legendary boots he was being asked to fill. His first task was to get Scotland through the play-off with Australia. Fergie appointed Walter Smith as his assistant, and a 0–0 draw in Australia after a 2–0 first-leg success at Hampden meant that Scotland were bound for Mexico.

Ferguson added Craig Brown, Archie Knox and Andy Roxburgh to his band of coaches and also enlarged the medical team. He did not want to leave anything to chance and even visited Sir Alf Ramsey to pick his brains about the management of a World Cup squad in Mexico. (As well as leading England to victory in the 1966 World Cup, Ramsey had also been in charge of the team for the 1970 World Cup in Mexico.) Sir Alf proved to be more than helpful, and Ferguson has never shunned from mentioning the willingness of the former England manager to help the Scotland squad.

This willingness to approach the ex-manager of the 'Auld Enemy' underlines just how much of a student of the game Sir Alex has always been and how meticulous he is in his preparation. He has always been keen to learn from others and has hungered for gems from anyone who could provide him with knowledge that he did not himself possess. He has never been a mildly interested student of football but, instead, a pupil with passion. Even as the temporary boss of the Scotland squad, Fergie was learning new tricks and the wealth of his experience and knowledge was being increased.

Craig Brown once recalled to me being a part of Fergie's coaching team for the 1986 World Cup. 'I was manager of Clyde at the time, and I was delighted when I was asked to join up,' he said. 'I had known Alex for some time, both as player and manager. We had played alongside each other as Scotland schoolboys. It was certainly good to link up with him for the challenge in Mexico, even though things did not turn out as we might have liked.'

Scotland were drawn in a tough group with Denmark, West Germany and Uruguay. Progressing to the next stage at the expense of any one of those sides was going to be a tall order. Although Denmark may have appeared to be the weakest side in the group on paper, they actually beat both West Germany and Uruguay, and defeated Scotland 1–0. However, had what seemed to be a perfectly good Roy Aitken goal not been ruled out for offside against the Danes in the opening group match, the whole complexion of the tournament might have changed for the Scots. A goalless draw against Uruguay eventually ended Scotland's interest in the tournament, but not before their match against West Germany.

'Alex was always very thorough in his preparation, and he even banned onlookers from the pre-match training,' said Craig. 'That was particularly so when we were preparing to face West Germany, because there was a question mark over Gordon Strachan's fitness. He had a niggling injury, and Ferguson wanted to test him fully to see if he could be included in the line-up.

'Berti Vogts was assistant to Franz Beckenbauer, manager of West Germany at the time, and, due to Ferguson's instructions, he was refused entry to the stadium where we were training. Not to be thwarted, Berti borrowed a Coca-Cola salesman's outfit and a drinks stall and was able to watch some of the Scotland workout unrecognised. He has ribbed Fergie about it a few times since.'

Strachan played and scored the opening goal, but the West German side fought back and eventually won 2–1. They admitted, though, that Scotland had given them their hardest game for quite some time.

The Scots returned home both disappointed and, according to the media, disappointing. 'Alex was severely criticised, which I thought was very harsh,' said Brown. 'I know the manager is always expected to carry the can – I have been there myself – but, as often happens, the expectations had been raised by the very people who were later the worst critics.

'Under the circumstances, the Scotland team had not disgraced their country, and the manager had worked hard to do his best to get through a very tough group. I cannot think of anyone else who would have put more into it and got better results.'

Ferguson was also disappointed, and in his autobiography, he blamed himself for not getting the team selection right for the Uruguay game, a match which could have made all the difference. In particular, he berated himself for not picking Aberdeen players Steve Archibald and Jim Bett because of a worry that he would be accused of showing favouritism.

Not being a man who takes defeat readily, he was relieved to get back on Scottish soil and start to look once again at how he was going to plot further success for Aberdeen. In terms of trophies, his short spell as Scotland boss had been fruitless, but for the man himself, it was certainly worthwhile as he had learned much more about a different kind of management, a management which gives you only limited access to your players, some of whom are more loyal to their clubs than their country. He also added to his knowledge of facing foreign opposition and the miscellany of styles and ploys that could be encountered.

Ferguson knew that, for the time being at least, his spell in charge of the Scottish side was over, and the SFA appointed Andy Roxburgh to become the new national manager. It would be unfair to say that Roxburgh was overly influenced by Ferguson, although they had been teammates at Falkirk. However, the new Scotland boss did admire Fergie's determination to succeed. 'He has always had a very infectious will to win,' Roxburgh said. 'I remember it when we were both playing, and it was evident when he was with the Scottish national side as well as with Aberdeen and with Manchester United. Of course, he did not win them all, nobody does, but the desire and hunger for success never lessens.'

The relationship between Roxburgh and Ferguson continued

over the next few years, the two men regularly communicating when the Scotland boss wanted to pick Manchester United players for the national side. However, it was with Roxburgh's successor Craig Brown that Fergie had a stronger influence. Brown was assistant to Roxburgh but was later to become Scotland manager himself.

Brown was raised in Glasgow during the Second World War, just as Ferguson was, yet there are few obvious similarities between the two, and they are like chalk and cheese in terms of personality. While Sir Alex has often been described as a fiery Scot, Brown has always been calm and well mannered. Brown had a very good education and is a qualified school teacher. Like Fergie, he played for Rangers for a short time but was more successful with Dundee and later at Falkirk, though that was before Alex Ferguson became a player there.

A knee problem put paid to Brown's playing career prematurely. He had always taken an interest in coaching, and even though teaching became his full-time profession for a while, Brown gradually became more and more involved in football until the time came when he had to make a choice. 'I was asked if I would like to become part-time assistant to Willie McLean, who was manager of Motherwell, having taken over from Ian St John,' said Brown. 'I was very happy to be asked and had little hesitation in accepting. I think I learned more from Willie than from any other manager, although you do learn from each and every one you come into contact with.'

The football merry-go-round throws up some interesting connections. When Billy McNeill left Clyde to become manager of Aberdeen, he recommended Craig Brown for the job of manager that he was leaving behind. Brown was approached, and before long, he was being hailed as the new boss of Clyde. The club was in the bottom division at the time, and the new manager's mission was to get them out of it. Brown did so at the first attempt, and as champions of the old Second Division, Clyde were on the march.

There were ups and downs during Brown's time at the club, but his own reputation was burgeoning and he was approached to become assistant to Jock Stein with the Scottish national side. It was a tempting offer, but Brown felt that he was not ready to go full time at that stage in his life and politely declined.

Brown certainly encountered Alex Ferguson during this time. By now, Fergie had become boss of Aberdeen, and Clyde were drawn to play against the Dons in the fourth round of the 1983–84 Scottish Cup. During a radio interview which Brown gave, knowing that Ferguson was listening, he claimed that they would be using a Dunlop ball and that the pitch had not been rolled for three weeks. The choice of ball referred to a comment Ferguson had made some months earlier. The phone rang immediately with Fergie breathing fire at the other end telling Brown not to use a Dunlop ball and to make sure that the pitch was rolled.

'No way, Alex,' said Brown. 'We're the home team.'

Home teams are entitled to use all kinds of advantage-seeking ploys, and Brown knew how to upset his old pal and adversary. Aberdeen still won 2–0, but Brown almost mentally outwitted Fergie. There were no lasting bad feelings, though, because Ferguson personally invited Brown to be one of his coaches when he took charge of the Scotland squad in 1986.

'I was delighted to be asked and willingly accepted,' said Brown. 'I was still at Clyde at the time, but the timing of the World Cup and the preparations fitted in perfectly. It was, of course, very exciting to be involved in the world's most spectacular sports tournament, but I think there was a little too much hype before we left Scotland. The media always talk up our chances, and, in some ways, I can understand that, but with the hype comes expectation and that can be hard to fulfil.

'When you consider that we were drawn in such a tough group against the likes of Denmark, Uruguay and West Germany, as it was then, Scotland were certainly the underdogs. We did not get past the first group stage, of course, and because of that, there was a lot of criticism of the manager, which I thought was very unfair. He had never talked up our chances, and he had been dropped in at the deep end.

'It was interesting to watch him in action as the boss, because he worked hard to prepare his team for each match and left nothing to chance. I thought he handled the disappointments well and never criticised his players for anything. He also handled the man management very well. It is always harder when you are not their club manager.'

Brown obviously enjoyed the experience of working alongside Ferguson and that must have contributed to his own achievements when he became Scotland's national manager and gave the country one of its most sustained spells of success. However, despite the obvious respect Brown has for Ferguson, when he was assistant to Roxburgh and the Scotland boss himself, his relationship with Sir Alex was not always plain sailing: 'Sometimes it can be very frustrating when you are in charge of the national team, or even one of the coaches, and you want to be able to pick your best team but you can't because club managers do not want to release them to you. I can understand it, because they don't want to risk injury to key players, but, having said that, we all have a job to do. More than one player has suddenly developed a "groin strain" which miraculously disappeared after an international and just in time for his next club match.

'When Andy was in charge, and likewise when I was in charge, there were occasions when things became a little heated between ourselves and Fergie. It was a little strange that having been an international manager himself he sometimes did not seem to understand the need for players to be released to their country. On the other hand, it is a tribute to his dedication to his club and his players that he wanted the best for them above all else.'

The uneasy relationship between club and international manager has existed for many years but has become even more prevalent in recent times when the number of matches played by national sides seems to have risen so dramatically. For this reason, the current Scotland boss Walter Smith, a friend to both Ferguson and Brown, has made a real effort to keep the club managers of his players on side. Especially at the beginning of his tenure, he forfeited a number of friendly matches and held squad training sessions instead. It was a shrewd manoeuvre that helped to get relationships going in the right direction.

Smith has always been a canny operator, and his move into management, eventually being appointed as the Scotland boss, seemed almost inevitable, because it always appeared that his leanings were more towards coaching at the highest level than playing at it. He was born in Lanark on 24 February 1948, and, like most boys his age, he began kicking a ball about the streets as soon as he could walk. He played at schools level and then for Ashfield Juniors, another club well known for finding and developing young football talent. Although he was a good player, Smith was not totally confident that he would actually manage to have a career in the game, so he became an apprentice electrician when he left school. It is amazing to think that all these years later he has the top football job in Scotland.

A right-sided defender, he was spotted by a scout for Dundee United and joined the club in November 1966. While others about him did not make the grade, Smith steadily earned his place in the first team and by 1970 was one of the regulars, remaining with United until September 1975 when he transferred to Dumbarton.

Throughout this time, Smith had taken a keen interest in

coaching, and after 18 months at Dumbarton, he returned to Tannadice as a player and youth coach. His last first-team match was in September 1980, but he stayed on as assistant to Jim McLean during a spell in which Dundee United won the championship and even reached the semi-finals of the European Cup.

Smith's coaching prowess had not gone unnoticed by those at the SFA, and while he was still with Dundee United, he also became coach of Scotland's Under-18 side in 1978. His young team went on to win the European Youth Championship in 1982. 'It was a good grounding for me,' Smith said. 'I had always been interested in coaching and the techniques used, as well as the day-to-day running of a football club. Coaching at international level called for a different approach in some ways, but the aim was always the same – to get the best from your players, to help them get the best from themselves and the game, and to win the next match.'

Having stepped up to coach the Scotland Under-21 side, Smith was an established part of the Scotland set-up when he was asked to assist Alex Ferguson with the national senior side in Mexico in 1986. 'Walter Smith is one of the best coaches around, and I consider him to be a good and reliable friend,' said Ferguson when he was asked to comment on Smith's appointment as Scotland boss. Fergie was also delighted to have had Smith as his assistant and confidant when he took on the role of Scotland manager himself. Many of the decisions taken during Mexico '86 were thrashed out by the two men before being announced.

'It was quite a year, really, because the World Cup provided for an amazing experience,' said Smith. 'You have to be part of it to truly appreciate it, but it was great to be there, although we were very disappointed with our results. Alex did his best, but the odds were stacked against him with some players unavailable, a very difficult group and some [refereeing] decisions during games which certainly did Scotland no favours at all.

'I don't think criticism was deserved. People may have different opinions, but unless they can be put into practice, nothing can ever be proven. I have to say that observing Fergie's approach to everything at close hand makes you realise how thorough he is and how he gets the best out of his players. If you look back, you will see that his teams have rarely performed badly for more than a week or two before bouncing back. That is the sign of a good manager who knows how to motivate.'

After the 1986 World Cup, Walter was invited by Graeme Souness to become part of his new regime at Ibrox, a regime which worked wonders and brought about a Rangers revolution that took the club out of the shadow of Celtic and into the limelight of British football. The combination of two men who had experienced working with Fergie proved to be an irresistible force. 'Graeme had obviously learned from various others, including Alex, used some of what he had learned and combined it all with his own ideas on how things should be done. Like Fergie, he certainly led by example,' said Smith. 'It was a historic period in the history of the club, and I was very happy to be a part of it.'

When Souness finally left Rangers in April 1991, Smith was the obvious choice to take over. With the new man at the helm, the club continued one of the most successful spells in its recent history, winning the Scottish championship six times in succession (making a record-equalling nine in a row when added to the three won by Smith's predecessor), the Scottish Cup and the Scottish League Cup three times each, and doing the domestic Treble in 1993. It was little wonder that Smith was awarded an OBE in 1997.

All good things have to come to an end, though, and Smith eventually left Rangers to become the manager of Everton in

1998. Great things were expected, but the formula which had worked so well at Ibrox could not be repeated at Goodison, where the club was troubled off the pitch and lacked confidence on it. Walter gave it his best shot but success eluded him, and he and Everton parted company in March 2002.

Ferguson and Smith have sparked a few times over the years, but, in general, they are the best of friends, and it seemed appropriate when Walter was appointed as temporary assistant to Fergie at Old Trafford for a few months in 2004. Both men knew it was a short-term arrangement, but it suited them at the time, and Ferguson knew Smith well enough to be confident that he was totally on his wavelength. With similar backgrounds and similar playing and coaching careers, both men knew what it was like to carry the weight of big-club management.

'It was good to be working with Alex again, and I enjoyed it very much,' Smith recalled. 'He had lost none of his will to win nor his sense of humour, two vital ingredients when you are a football manager.'

Ferguson's sense of humour was tested by his former national-team assistants during the 1994 World Cup in the USA. 'I had been watching a match with Walter,' Brown said. 'It was a sunny day, and Walter had bought himself a genuine Stetson to wear. When the game was over, we bumped into Fergie, who talked to me but obviously did not recognise Walter under the Stetson. I seized on the opportunity and introduced him as an American friend of mine. Fergie shook hands, Walter put on an accent and kept his head down until he could not stand it any longer and revealed who he was.'

That must have been one of the most bizarre meetings ever of Scotland managers past, present and future. It also briefly reunited three men who have had a major influence on Scottish football. Although Ferguson may not have had the best of times when he was temporarily in charge of the national side, he has undoubtedly made his mark on Brown and Smith. And his influence on Smith, in particular, could one day prove to be of great benefit to the supporters of the Scotland national team.

However, it was not just the coaches who worked with Ferguson during the World Cup in Mexico who benefited from the experience. Although he never played for Manchester United, Aberdeen, St Mirren or East Stirling, Graeme Souness did play for Scotland and freely admits that he found his contact with Fergie to be influential, even though their time together was limited: 'I don't think you could come into any sort of contact with Sir Alex Ferguson without being influenced by him, even as an opponent.'

Graeme Souness was one of those players you just had to have on your side. He was swift and fearless in the tackle, prepared to take on defenders, able to cross and pass accurately, and could even pop up in the middle of a penalty-box mêlée to score a valuable goal on occasion. From the moment he began his career, Graeme Souness was never going to be a player you overlooked.

The two men were probably at their closest when Souness was captain of Scotland and Fergie was first of all assistant to Jock Stein and then national team boss for the 1986 World Cup. Their relationship was not without its controversies, Ferguson dropping Souness from the team for the group match against Uruguay. 'I have often said that Fergie is the only manager who ever dropped me,' Souness once told me when I interviewed him. 'It is true, except that when I was player–manager at Rangers, I dropped myself a couple of times. I am proud of the fact that from when I was growing up as a schoolboy in Edinburgh right through to playing for Tottenham, Middlesbrough, Liverpool, Sampdoria and Scotland, I was only ever dropped once and that was by Fergie.'

It might sound as if Souness is bitter about that one blot on his footballing CV, but he isn't. He is almost proud of the fact that he was dropped by a manager whom he considers to be the best: 'When you talk about the managerial greats of all time, Fergie has to be one of the first names you would think of. He was brilliantly successful with Aberdeen, and very few managers do it all again, plus some, with another club. Fergie did.'

When Fergie became Jock Stein's assistant in 1984, Souness was already a long-established first-choice player for the national side. The more Ferguson saw of him, both in training and during matches, the more he appreciated his qualities. However, when it came to the World Cup, some tough decisions had to be made, especially in the selection of the side to face Uruguay. Souness had not been playing well. He had a tremendous record as player and captain of Scotland, but at the age of 33, and with his new job as player–manager of Rangers looming, it was plain that he was no longer an automatic choice. Leaving him out was still a major decision, though, because his no-nonsense approach would be useful against opponents like Uruguay. It would almost certainly be the last World Cup Graeme Souness would ever take part in as a player, so there were some sentimental factors to take into consideration as well. However, Ferguson was not one to be influenced by such things, and Souness was duly left out of the team.

'I knew that it was likely that I would not be picked, but the way Fergie handled it was a lesson in man management,' said Souness. 'He personally came to my room to tell me and to explain the reasons behind his decision. It must have taken a lot for him to do that, and a lesser manager might have just announced the team and said nothing to any individual.' Fergie had been down that road himself, of course, when he was dropped by Dunfermline for the 1965 cup final.

Although Souness knew that Ferguson was a formidable character, he fully supported the appointment of Fergie as temporary manager after Jock Stein's sudden death. 'When Jock died, the obvious person to take over was Fergie,' Souness said. 'He didn't really want the job, but knowing that Scotland needed someone in charge, he made himself available. I don't think he has ever been very keen on being the manager of a national side, although the challenge would appeal to him. I believe he prefers the day-to-day coaching and contact with his players, rather than just getting them every now and then.

'Taking Scotland to Mexico was thrust upon him rather than being his choice, and it was a tough time for everyone, since the loss of Jock had left a tremendous gap that nobody could have really filled, and the group we found ourselves in could hardly have been more difficult.

'I think it is only when you become a manager yourself that you really appreciate what being in charge of a side really means. It is a huge responsibility, and if you are in charge of a squad that has the hopes of the nation pinned on it and the focus of the world on it in football's biggest tournament, that pressure must be immense.'

Although Scotland's World Cup campaign fizzled out to nothing, Souness still learned something from his boss and took some of the Fergie approach into his own management career: he had the same cavalier attitude, aggressive at times but charming at others; he too roasted his players within an inch of their lives; and he also demanded nothing but the absolute highest standards.

Souness was also willing to break with convention, most notably when he signed Mo Johnston, who was not only a Catholic but a former Celtic hero. Although the player had looked set to return to Parkhead after a spell with Nantes, Souness stepped in and secured his signature. The Rangers manager adopted the same set-jaw approach as Sir Alex and was determined not to let religious divides stand between himself and a player who he felt

Fergie in a Dunfermline shirt – about to conquer the world.

Alex and Jim Baxter skip training with Rangers.

Celtic stars look accusingly at Fergie. Who me? Surely not?

They think it's all over – and it was. The final whistle blows, and
Aberdeen have won the European Cup-Winners' Cup.

Fergie and Jock Stein just before that fateful final whistle.

It's tense as Fergie and Walter Smith try to mastermind
Scottish success at the 1986 World Cup.

Simply the best – Fergie and Eric Cantona pick up yet more awards.

To the victors, the spoils. Fergie and the boys after winning the
European Champions League final against Bayern Munich.

Fergie at a press conference – relaxed and in control.

The sight all his
players want to see –
a thumbs-up from
Fergie.

The FA headquarters are that way – Fergie shows Steve McClaren
where he is headed.

Happy days: Fergie and Roy share a joke.

Sir Alex, Mike Phelan and Walter Smith in conference at Old Trafford.

Reunited at Ibrox: Fergie and Alex McLeish.

Fergie celebrates, Gordon Strachan doesn't. United against Southampton was, at one point, a former Dons reunion.

Back to back but still United. Fergie and the man who may one day replace him – Mark Hughes.

could make a positive difference to his team. The signing of Johnston caused uproar in Glasgow, but Souness rose above the furore and proved his point by putting Rangers back in the Old Firm driving seat.

It was not long before the erstwhile colleagues were locking horns in the Scottish Premier Division as managers. 'When I took over as manager of Rangers, Fergie was still in charge of Aberdeen and one of my earliest games was against his Aberdeen side,' said Souness. 'I was actually injured in that game, and I did not have the powers of recovery I once had, so, despite trying to get back, it was really time to hang up my boots. Matches against Aberdeen always had an extra edge. There is a bit of history between the two clubs, nothing like the Old Firm rivalry, of course, but still an edge, and especially since Aberdeen had been turned into quite a forceful outfit by Alex at that time.

'He is a wily opponent, and it seemed strange to be picking a team and playing myself against the man who I had called boss just a couple of months earlier. It was not long afterwards that he became manager of Manchester United and Rangers went on to recapture the championship.'

Souness was himself earmarked as a possible manager of Manchester United during the time when Michael Knighton attempted to take over the club. It was pre-1990 and Alex Ferguson's future as boss was the subject of much debate. Knighton's plan was to make major changes at the club, including the appointment of Graeme Souness as successor to Ferguson.

United's loss was Liverpool's gain when Souness became manager of the Merseyside outfit following the surprise resignation of Kenny Dalglish. It was a blow to Rangers but a logical step for Souness, because his relationship with the Scottish media was becoming worse and the thought of going back to the club where he had been so successful as a player was very inviting.

It was April 1991 when Graeme Souness drove back into the Anfield car park. Behind him were three Scottish league championships – and another about to be clinched – various other trophies and a catalogue of exciting events and signings which had turned Rangers back into the mightiest force in Scottish football.

Much was expected of him when he returned to Liverpool, but there was not the same drive at Anfield that he had experienced as a player there the previous decade. During that time, there had been a tremendous passion that carried players and supporters alike from one triumph to another. Souness himself had been captain of one of the European Cup-winning sides. What he returned to was a pale imitation of that time.

The thrill of taking on the job at the club which had meant so much to him soon evaporated with the realisation that Dalglish had left at just the right time. Turning the club round without treading on toes was impossible. Dalglish had found it difficult to become boss of players who had been his teammates for some time, and the bite had gone out of the club. Souness had inherited a decaying institution, and when he tried to make changes, he was immediately criticised by some of the old-stagers, who thought he should leave things alone. It was an impossible situation and probably contributed to his having to go into hospital for heart surgery.

Obviously that was a traumatic time for him, but, again, he showed the same Scottish grit as Fergie by returning to work in time to sit on the bench at Wembley as Liverpool took on Sunderland in the FA Cup final in 1992. He had plotted their progress through the competition until undergoing surgery just before their semi-final success against Portsmouth. He was determined not to allow a near-death encounter stop him from witnessing his team's effort in the final.

Ronnie Moran had taken charge of the side during Graeme's

absence, and it was he who led the team out at Wembley. Souness kept a low profile. There had been some ill-feeling over his agreeing to be photographed in hospital after the semi-final victory by *The Sun*, which had made itself unpopular among Liverpool fans due to its coverage of the Hillsborough disaster in 1989.

Eventually, of course, came the parting of the ways, and Souness bowed out of Anfield. He took a year out of the game and was in no rush to return. However, the opportunity to become manager of Galatasaray was a challenge he could not resist, and he signed a one-year contract which was to see him lauded at the end of that season by the supporters after his side won the Turkish Cup by beating rivals Fenerbahçe. T-shirts hailing Souness could be seen all over Istanbul after that, but the call to return to England as manager of Southampton was too strong, and he turned down the opportunity to sign for another year in Turkey.

During his time at Southampton, the side did make progress, and the fans still talk about their historic 6–3 win over Manchester United, an occasion when Souness surely outwitted Alex Ferguson, even using some of his own tactics against him. 'There are great advantages in getting to know opposing managers well, because you know how they think, how they prepare and how you can match them or even beat them,' Souness said. 'The game still has to be won on the pitch, of course, but you can still do your bit as manager.'

From Southampton, Souness had brief and forgettable spells as coach at Torino and Benfica before returning to take charge of Blackburn Rovers. Then, amid more controversy, he became manager of Newcastle United, where he walked into another arena of high expectation. Things looked to be going well in the North-east, especially when Michael Owen was signed from Real Madrid, but a long list of injuries to key players scuppered any progress, and Souness was sacked in February 2006.

Graeme Souness has rarely been far away from controversy, on or off the pitch. The same could be said about Sir Alex Ferguson, but they both share a common ability to withstand all kinds of ups and downs and criticisms which might make lesser men crack. Both men are also philosophical about life and both have a very good, and often needed, sense of humour. But it is in football terms that the real similarities can be seen, and Souness has admitted that he has directly copied elements of Ferguson's methods. 'He is extremely resilient,' said Souness of Ferguson. 'He has had the most high-profile job in football as manager of Manchester United, but even before that at Aberdeen, he took on a massive challenge. He had to break the stranglehold of the Old Firm and take the Dons to a new level, something they had rarely experienced before.

'He did that by getting a siege mentality into his players. Shankly used to do the same. He would have them believing that the world was against them and it was up to them to fight back and prove to everyone that they deserved respect. Fergie did the same. He told his players that the big clubs of Glasgow looked down their noses at Aberdeen, as did the media. He got them fired up enough to do something about it, and, at the same time, it was a unifying technique which worked brilliantly.

'He has done the same thing at Manchester United, and even at the height of success, he will make statements saying that referees are against them, other supporters hate them and that the rest of football wants to give them a good beating. It pulls his squad closer together, and it makes them all the more determined to go out there and put on a great performance.

'I have used the same technique myself, and it worked perfectly at Rangers, where I assured everyone that Celtic thought they were on a perch that nobody would ever knock them off. I sent my players out to prove that Rangers was not the club of yesteryear but of today and tomorrow. It is a ploy used by many and works well. Fergie has developed it into an art form.'

Souness came into conflict with Ferguson on occasion when their respective teams faced each other, but there is mutual respect between the two men, and Souness is the first to praise Ferguson: 'Sir Alex is without a doubt the top manager in British football today and has made himself a legend even while he is still in the game. He will retire some day, and perhaps it will then be realised even more what he has done for Manchester United and the game as a whole. He could be considered as the greatest manager the game has ever seen because of his enormous success with two ailing clubs which he turned into the best in Europe in their day.

'His knowledge of the game, his man management, his tactical approach and the respect he has is second to none, and he is always willing to have a chat and will be quite open with any advice he feels might help another manager.'

Graeme Souness has openly admitted that he has learned from Sir Alex, so that definitely places him among the beneficiaries of the Fergie legacy. Who knows where that might lead. While Souness was manager at Rangers, Walter Smith was his No. 2. Perhaps one day the roles might be reversed with Souness assisting in a Scotland revival and putting to good use the knowledge and experience that he has gained from his contact with and observations of Sir Alex. It might not have worked out at Newcastle, but we are unlikely to have seen the last of Graeme Souness on the touchline.

While Sir Alex Ferguson would be the first to refute that he has had much influence on the Scottish national team, there is little doubt that he has played a part in its recent history and could yet play a part in its future.

6

OLD TRAFFORD

WHEN ALEX FERGUSON RETURNED FROM THE WORLD CUP IN MEXICO, HE WAS 44 years old and had already amassed an incredible football legacy as player, club boss and now international manager. As he returned to Pittodrie, it is quite likely that there were those who wondered what, if anything, he could achieve next. Some managers have a bright start to their careers but then become also-rans for the rest of their years. For Alex Ferguson, the best was yet to come, a line pinched from a well-known song best performed by one of his favourite singers, Frank Sinatra.

Around that time, Aberdeen became resigned to the fact that they would be losing their manager sooner or later. The pack of chasing clubs continued to increase. Just a few months before the World Cup, Arsenal had made a second attempt to enlist him, but after a discussion, he turned them down. How football history would have been changed if he had accepted. Perhaps Arsène Wenger would have become manager of Manchester United!

As the 1986–87 season began, Ron Atkinson was still in the

creaking manager's chair at Old Trafford, and Alex Ferguson was still in the hot seat at Pittodrie. It wouldn't stay that way for long. Archie Knox joined Fergie as assistant manager at Aberdeen, but it was hardly worth his while to unpack his bags. The rumours of Ron Atkinson's departure from Old Trafford were matched by the further rumours of Alex Ferguson's imminent arrival. It became the talk of both Manchester and Aberdeen, although those directly concerned were not even at the preliminary-discussions stage.

As Aberdeen started their season with a string of successes, Manchester United began with some very poor results, and it seemed that the unthinkable could be on the cards: the possibility that the most famous club in the world would be relegated from the top division. With United faltering on the pitch and the rumours reaching fever pitch, Fergie did at last receive a phone call asking him to talk to Martin Edwards, then chairman of Manchester United. He agreed and a meeting was hastily arranged. At least that's the official story and the one told by Alex Ferguson, although it is rare in football for these things to take place so spontaneously. Other accounts suggest that United had been tracking Ferguson for some months. Ron Atkinson himself remembered a conversation between himself and Martin Edwards in March 1986 during which Ron had suggested standing down, even though United had not been having too bad a season. Ron also recalled that various obstructions were placed in his way when he tried to sign new players during his last couple of months in charge. It was as if the board did not want him to bring in any new personnel that might not suit his replacement.

Whatever the real story, there was definitely a meeting between the United directors and the man they wanted. It might have been a first meeting or it might have been the one which crossed the 't's and dotted the 'i's, but the outcome was the same either way.

Ron Atkinson left Manchester United while November was still in its early days, and Alex Ferguson was named as his replacement within a few hours. It required some soul searching by the Aberdeen boss, because he had been asked to stay by his chairman Dick Donald, who virtually offered to give Fergie the club in recognition of his achievements.

He had to consider his family, too, and how they might take to moving to England after spending their whole lives in Scotland up to that point. It was a big decision, and it even meant taking a pay cut, because Fergie's potential earnings with a successful Aberdeen side were greater than those with a struggling Manchester United team.

But the lure of taking charge of a club that had such an incredible history was extremely tempting. To fill the shoes once laced by Sir Matt Busby, to take on the challenge once reluctantly turned down by Jock Stein and to live the reality that others only dreamed about was just too good to refuse, and Ferguson therefore had to close his ears to the appeals of Aberdeen to stay on with them and focus on a new mission. Archie Knox was asked to take on the role of manager at Pittodrie, but he chose instead to join United alongside Fergie, and the two men embarked upon what was for both of them the biggest challenge of their lives.

It has been said that Ferguson did not know what he was letting himself in for – that he was bewitched by the Manchester United image. He has admitted that he did not realise how much repair was needed at the club when he arrived. For example, Ron Atkinson had always been very relaxed about training and preferred instead to build his team's psychological approach to matches. It was a formula that had worked for him in the past but did not seem to be having the desired effect on his players in the run up to his sacking. Fergie immediately changed all of that. He ordered players in earlier, and he changed the training methods dramatically. The new manager knew that a complete overhaul of training, conduct and attitude was necessary. He has since revealed his shock at seeing how unfit the United players seemed to be and how their attitude lacked any sort of killer instinct. They were so relaxed as to be complacent even in the face of defeat. That was not at all the Fergie recipe for success.

After losing 2–0 to Oxford in his first game in charge, Ferguson must have wondered what he had done. He discovered that most of the senior players had been at a farewell party thrown by the outgoing Ron Atkinson less than 48 hours before the clash with Oxford and that much of the Old Trafford culture was to do with social life rather than football life.

The following Monday was a good day to get started, and before training commenced, Ferguson addressed all the players, explaining his expectations and telling them that they would be on a greater fitness quest from then on. He also told them that he expected their social life would, in future, come a distant second behind their dedication and commitment to the club. He had little else to say, and he kept everything calm and almost low key. But that was just the start, and it was not long before his new players discovered how much emphasis Fergie put on fitness and stamina. They worked like they had not worked for some seasons.

Some players loved it, while others found it all a bit of a culture shock. Ferguson was impervious to their opinions; he and Archie Knox knew what they wanted and that was all that mattered at that stage. 'We wanted team spirit,' Knox said shortly afterwards. 'That was mostly going to have to come from the younger players who had been through the youth training system and were dedicated to the club. Rome wasn't built in a day, and we knew there was not going to be any quick fix, so Alex went about making new rules and seeing who was prepared to go along with the changes. There were young players waiting in the wings to replace those who did not go along with the changes.'

Manchester United were a big club and some people perhaps imagined that the Reds' manager could just nip to the soccer supermarket at any time and buy new recruits, but it was not that simple. Ron Atkinson had mostly balanced the books well with his purchases and sales, but it had been necessary, because United did not have the bottomless pit of money everyone supposed. They had to budget like everyone else, and there was little in the transfer pot. Fergie had to make changes without a burgeoning cheque book at his disposal.

The players in the first-team squad when Ferguson arrived at the club included Gordon Strachan, of course, Paul McGrath, Mike Duxbury, Chris Turner, Peter Davenport, Arthur Albiston, Kevin Moran, Graeme Hogg, Remi Moses, Peter Barnes, Frank Stapleton, Jesper Olsen, Clayton Blackmore, Norman Whiteside and Bryan Robson. On paper, there was a lot of talent there, but it had to be harnessed and disciplined. The players had to be turned into a fighting force that would not only lift United out of the doldrums of the lower reaches of the First Division but would also put the club back where its legion of supporters firmly believed that it deserved to be – at the top of the league.

Alex Ferguson must have seriously reflected on the task that was before him. He was well used to the rigours of club management by then, and he had even been manager of his country, but Manchester United was something else. However, he was well equipped for the job in hand. As a player, he had worked for a variety of managers and had gained something from each of them. He had learned much about man management or the lack of it. He knew about tactics, ploys, playing players out of position, harnessing players who really needed to be allowed to express themselves. He knew about psychology and could inspire players, his coaching team, the directors, the commercial staff and, most importantly, the supporters. His success rate was proven, which is why he was pursued and offered what has been described as the biggest job in domestic football.

Alex was also familiar with dealing with directors; he had seen enough erratic behaviour from them even before he agreed to join Manchester United. He knew how to argue with them, cajole them into his way of thinking and to appeal to their sense of commitment when he wanted to go over his transfer budget. Back at East Stirling, he had been given a budget of £2,000 for transfers and not enough players to field a complete side. Here at Old Trafford, there were enough players, but pound for pound the budget was not much better. He would have to call upon all his guile and wheel and deal in the transfer market.

He was also proud, had passion and possessed a great hunger for success. Despite his achievements so far in Scottish football, Alex Ferguson remained as keen as a beginner. He loved a challenge, and returning Manchester United to their glory days was perhaps the biggest challenge he had yet faced.

All that knowledge and experience, all those contacts, had been amassed as a treasure chest of football wisdom to be used for the benefit of those paying his wages and cheering on his team. And with this depth of experience and expertise behind him, Fergie rolled up his sleeves and got on with the job. He was not there to win any popularity contests but to put Manchester United back on the trail of triumph. Results on the pitch had to improve rapidly, and they did. The extra training, adjustment of attitudes and introduction of a little bit of fear gave the players an extra edge. By the end of the season, Manchester United finished in a mid-table position, and everyone breathed a sigh of relief. Everyone except Fergie, that is.

He knew he was going to have to change some members of the squad in order for further progress to be made. He also knew that Manchester United had a great tradition and reputation for bringing through youngsters from what is arguably the best youth-training scheme in the business – this would have to continue. As a result, he kept a close eye on the talent that was being nurtured at the club. Fergie's original plan might have been short-term survival, but in the long term, he wanted to build a team capable of going even further than he had at Aberdeen. There was a hunger among the fans for United to once again be champions of England and, indeed, Europe. Alex Ferguson shared their hunger.

The following season, the promise was almost fulfilled as United lost only five of their forty league fixtures. Runners-up was great, and a big improvement, but it still wasn't the real thing. Finishing second to Liverpool was hard to bear for the United fans, and dropping out of the FA Cup in a controversial fifth-round tie at Arsenal also didn't help their moods.

Players left and others came in, not all of them the wisest of choices. For example, Mal Donaghy was brought in to bolster a flagging defence, but he was nearing the end of his career, and while it could be argued that he admirably fulfilled what was required of him, it was only a short-term answer. And although Dion Dublin's chances of a glittering career at Old Trafford may have been ruined by injury, did he ever actually have what it takes to be a Manchester United hero?

Of the players Fergie wanted but was unable to get at that time, he has always said that his biggest disappointment was not signing Paul Gascoigne. As far as Ferguson was concerned, the deal was done and only needed a signature. The next thing he knew, Gazza had gone to Tottenham.

Ferguson was reminded more than once that while there was sympathy from the board that the manager's rebuilding programme needed new players while the youngsters were still progressing, they simply did not have the money to finance a quick fix. Having said that, there were some new arrivals at Old Trafford, among them Brian McClair, who was to prove to be a great servant of the club; Lee Sharpe, who had tremendous potential but never seemed to get his head in order; and Steve Bruce, a player who earned the undying respect of the United fans. There was also the return of a United hero in Mark Hughes, who was delighted to pull on the red shirt again.

Ferguson was clearly picking his players very carefully, another skill that those around him would take on board. The most recent season at Birmingham City is perhaps a poor example, but prior to that, Steve Bruce showed that he had inherited some of his former manager's guile for signing players. For example, the signing of Robbie Savage was a master stroke because Bruce knew he was buying someone with aggression and a will to win – two qualities Birmingham desperately needed. Losing him to Blackburn must have been a major blow. Unfortunately, other players who had been carefully selected also moved on, and decisions to replace them seem to have been clouded by events behind the scenes. Certainly, the Birmingham City side of 2005–06 did not appear to have the same Steve Bruce stamp, the one he inherited from Fergie.

Back at Old Trafford, there was renewed hope for the 1988–89 season. Alex Ferguson had made a profound statement in an interview during the summer. 'This isn't just a job to me, it is a mission,' he said. 'I want to be here for the rest of my career. We will get there, and when we do, life will change dramatically for Liverpool and the rest of football.' Whether it was bravado or the honest words of a man with a solid belief, we shall never really know, but, as it turned out, it was quite prophetic and nobody can now say that he was wrong. However, despite the optimism, the season fizzled into nothing with United finishing in 11th position, almost back where they had started when Fergie arrived.

The ailing support was also a worry, and at the end of the

season, the visit of Wimbledon saw only 23,268 turn up at Old Trafford. Wimbledon were hardly the most glamorous of sides, but when you consider that much larger crowds have turned up to see the likes of Exeter in happier days at the Theatre of Dreams, the growing disillusionment of that time becomes apparent.

Success brings with it the burden of criticism when things go wrong, and Manchester United have never been short of those willing to criticise, as anyone ever connected with the club will testify. Align yourself with the Old Trafford outfit and you are immediately cast into a goldfish bowl made from magnifying glass. The critics began to rub their hands with delight as Fergie struggled to achieve his goal. There was even talk of him returning to Scotland, where he had been successful before as a big fish in a small pond.

Criticism is seldom delicate, and those in the media often try to outdo one other in both rumourmongering and vitriolic aspersions. There were numerous rumours of rifts between the manager and the board, which both parties were quick to deny. However, while Kenny Dalglish at Liverpool and George Graham at Arsenal were smiling, Fergie's teeth became more clenched.

Although Ferguson had been disappointed when he arrived at the club that the youth system for which United had once been so famous had been allowed to fall into a state of neglect, he worked hard with the young players, knowing that they could bring future success. And his efforts to engage more scouts and woo smaller clubs from both near and far to inform United of any talent they discovered soon paid off.

It was a tip-off that led to him signing one of the club's modern heroes. The young player was actually attached to Manchester City and had played for England schoolboys, even though he was Welsh. Brian Kidd went along to see him in action and urged Ferguson to make the talented young winger a United player. City were asked if they had plans to sign him, but they revealed that they didn't, so he was free to join Manchester United. That young player was Ryan Giggs, and he has been a star since the first moment he pulled on the famous shirt.

This was all part of building for the future, but the present was still a nagging problem, and the critics continued to nip at the heels of the manager. And not all of them were media commentators. A section of United supporters were also keen on showing him the red card and suggested that he take an early bath back in Aberdeen.

Something dramatic was needed to restore the fans' faith; perhaps the 1989–90 season would be the turning point. However, things started badly and league form was inconsistent; once again, the 'heads must roll' brigade were having a field day. Fergie must have been tearing out his hair at that stage. He had brought in stars like Neil Webb, Paul Ince, Gary Pallister and Danny Wallace, but they still seemed far removed from being a championship side.

A 5–1 hiding by Manchester City looked like it would be the final straw. It might well have been if there had been an obvious replacement. The United board have always denied that they ever considered sacking Ferguson, but it must surely have crossed their minds after such a humiliating defeat by their neighbours from Maine Road.

The press had a field day and various names were put forward, the most likely being Howard Kendall, who had experience with a big club and knew about success. Kendall had his own personal issues to resolve, though, and taking charge of United at that stage would have probably been a mistake for all concerned.

The weeks went by and things did not get any better. It seemed only a matter of time before drastic action would be taken to change the fortunes of the club. At least progress in the FA Cup was some small consolation. If United could only harness those displays and put them into their weekly First Division commitments, the story would have been so much better. But they didn't. They rose to the cup occasions and continued to plod through the league fixtures.

Finishing 13th in the table meant that United had experienced their worst league position since the arrival of Alex Ferguson. Who was to say that Ron Atkinson would not ultimately have done better? Some critics asked that question, pointing to the fact that Big Ron had at least won the FA Cup for United.

The criticism was put on hold, however, when United reached the final of the world's oldest cup competition and Fergie was able to lead out his team in the mighty Wembley Stadium, his first ever visit as a manager. Few gave Crystal Palace much chance of success against United, but they almost turned Fergie's day into a nightmare when substitute Ian Wright scored twice to turn a 2–1 deficit into a 3–2 lead. That could have been the end of the road for Fergie: defeat by Crystal Palace at Wembley would have been too much for the United fans and possibly the board to handle.

It took just one spark to save the day, and it came from Mark Hughes, nicknamed Sparky by his former boss Ron Atkinson and certainly living up to the title. The minutes were ticking away when he popped up to hit his second goal of the game and force a replay.

Back at Wembley five days later, there was no room for error, and this time United sealed victory to the delight of the fans and the joy and relief of the manager. But again there had been criticism, and Fergie had been vilified by the press for dropping Jim Leighton after his erratic performance in the first game.

It seemed that nobody appreciated what a tough decision that had been for the manager. He had known Leighton for years, having been his boss at Aberdeen and in the Scotland squad, and here he was having to break the bad news that the goalkeeper was having to give up his place in the Wembley replay to Les Sealey. Leighton was not happy, and the FA Cup celebrations were somewhat spoiled by the media getting on Fegie's case and portraying him as the wicked Uncle Abanazer of the FA Cup panto.

That apart, United had at last won something, and the FA Cup was not to be sniffed at, especially as it opened the door to the competition which had won Fergie fame and glory with Aberdeen – the European Cup-Winners' Cup. As for Jim Leighton, to this day he has never truly forgiven Alex Ferguson for making him the scapegoat for United being forced into a replay in the 1990 FA Cup final. Ferguson has at times spoken highly of his former goalkeeper and at other times has been less than complimentary. Whatever his true thoughts on his ex-player, the decision to drop Leighton was made and no amount of discussion afterwards was going to change the fact – the manager always has the last word and has to live with his decisions, something that Fergie has been more than happy to do throughout his career.

During the 1990–91 season, United showed growing confidence and a marked league improvement. Fergie's men finished the season in sixth place but that might have been even better had it not been for the distraction of their involvement in two cup finals. There was certainly less talk of Fergie getting the sack, but the newspaper men were still kept busy when a famous brawl between United and Arsenal saw both clubs fined, United docked a point and Arsenal docked two points.

That season also saw the debut of Ryan Giggs, who had developed in the youth side under Fergie's watchful eye. However, the manager's man management was once again called into question because of his handling of the teenage star. Everyone wanted to have a piece of this new young maestro, and there was not a journalist in Britain who would not have given his drinking arm to get an interview with him. But Fergie shielded him, preferring to keep his young protégé away from the limelight. Those who were thwarted in their attempt to reach him immediately said that Fergie was being too protective and that he had his own commercial interests in the player. This was patently not the case but perhaps demonstrated another important managerial lesson: even when your team is winning on the pitch, it doesn't mean that you will win off it.

In the League Cup, there was a little twist of irony as United reached the final and were pitched against Second Division side Sheffield Wednesday, whose manager at the time was a fired-up Ron Atkinson. He would have loved nothing more than to beat United and prove a point, although nobody thought that was going to happen. But on the day, Wednesday were the better side, winning by the only goal of the match. Ferguson blamed himself for not getting his team selection right, but he also had a few choice words to say about the referee. Ron Atkinson just beamed like the cat who got the cream.

Ferguson admitted that he did not get it right and that United were below par on the day. He has never taken things for granted, because there is no room for complacency in football, but Ferguson has often sailed near the wind, sometimes getting it wrong as he has chosen to rest important players or give experience to younger players in games that he considered to be fairly easy or unimportant. In the final against Wednesday, Fergie chose to leave out Mike Phelan, a decision which he later regretted since there was a lack of extra drive on the right side of midfield, something which Wednesday wisely exploited.

The League Cup final might also have provided a wake-up call because the next big game on the horizon was the European Cup-Winners' Cup final in Rotterdam. Barcelona were the opponents and could not have been better selected: they were a high-profile side and also the former club of Mark Hughes, who was keen to remind them of what they were missing.

On 15 May 1991, millions of fans watched as Manchester United turned their biggest corner yet. It rained quite heavily – just as it had done in Gothenburg when Aberdeen played Real Madrid – which favoured the British side, and Barcelona had no answer to Fergie's game plan. Even before the match began, Ferguson had scored a huge psychological coup over his opponents by having Sir Matt Busby lead the team from the coach into the stadium. It was the greatest gauntlet he could have thrown down, not only to the opposition but also to his own players. It was a reminder that they could go some way towards emulating the legends of the class of '68.

They did, too, and won 2–1. United fans were united in their joy, and the talk changed from Fergie's possible sacking to him being approached by Real Madrid to become their boss. That match made all the difference in the world to how the club and, in particular, Alex Ferguson were perceived. Fans started addressing him as Mr Ferguson again.

The only downside to that successful season was the sudden departure of Archie Knox, who appeared to have become a fixture alongside Fergie. The two had worked as a team at Pittodrie and for several years at Old Trafford, but when Walter Smith invited Archie to become his No. 2 at Rangers, there was no hesitation. He even left before the Cup-Winners' Cup final in Rotterdam when he could so easily have agreed to join Rangers immediately afterwards. There never has been an explanation for his sudden move. There was no great rift between the two men, and United were prepared to match the improved financial package offered by Rangers. But Archie had made up his mind, and there was no stopping him. Fergie was disappointed to lose his No. 2 but understood that once Knox had taken the decision, there was no going back. Ferguson learned another valuable lesson: nothing is for ever and not everything can be explained.

Brian Kidd was made Fergie's assistant in August 1991. It was not an instant promotion but one that the boss considered for some time. He knew Kidd's strengths, but he also knew his weaknesses and wondered if they could work together as cohesively as he had with Knox. But Kidd knew United, having been part of both the playing and coaching teams, and the decision was made.

The problem of who to appoint as United's new assistant manager was solved relatively easily but the conundrum of how to build on the European success and take the team to the next level was not so straightforward. Winning the European Super Cup by beating Red Star Belgrade was OK but did not set the world on fire. There was only one real target now and that was the league championship. United had not won the title for a quarter of a century, and the hunger pangs were turning into stomach cramps. They looked as if they might do it during that 1991–92 season, but a disappointing run-in meant that they had to take second place to a more resilient Leeds United side which Howard Wilkinson had coolly and tactically refined into a title-winning machine. Manchester fans did not want to concede that they had been pipped to the post by a better team, but the league table did not tell lies.

United were good value for second place and beat Nottingham Forest 1–0 to take the League Cup. However, they fell early in their defence of the European Cup-Winners' Cup and did not go beyond the fourth round of the FA Cup. Another highlight of the season was the winning of the FA Youth Cup. That might not seem terribly exciting, but when you look at some of the names of those playing for United, it takes on a whole new significance. The list of those who played included David Beckham, Ryan Giggs, Keith

Gillespie, Robbie Savage, Gary Neville, Nicky Butt and Paul Scholes, all of whom went on to become star players.

The performances of goalkeeper Peter Schmeichel, who had joined the club from Brøndby, were also a plus point of the 1991–92 season. The great Dane had presented a headache for his own management on the day that he signed for the club in August 1991. The press call had to be delayed for a short time as the jersey and gloves given to him were too small. Nobody realised just how big he really was and certainly nobody realised how much of a giant he was going to become at Old Trafford.

He proved to be a super signing by Alex Ferguson, who had watched him while on foreign trips. It was a long way from East Stirling when a fistful of dollars on the table made all the difference to a signature. Now, Fergie was in a world of agents, accountants, directors and solicitors, and a lesser mortal might have been overawed. But Ferguson's experience of negotiating as a trades union representative proved invaluable. He had learned how to talk to people and how to deal with high-stake situations, lessons that he was able to put to good use.

The stakes were then raised even higher as the Premiership was born in 1992. It was an exciting time to be in football, but it was not a place for the faint-hearted, especially for managers. Increased money and television coverage meant that there were greater expectations, and managers knew they had to deliver and deliver quickly otherwise the board and the growing army of football-club shareholders would be demanding a public execution.

At the end of the 1991–92 season, Ferguson spoke to each of his players and told them that what they had achieved thus far was great but that they were on the verge of something even more wonderful. They had the opportunity to take the title and create a piece of history by being the first team to win the Premiership. Some players would have taken that as the boss just giving them something to think about during the summer, while others knew that, even though he spoke calmly, Fergie was deadly serious about the prospects for the new 1992–93 season.

Unfortunately, the start of the season was not quite as explosive as United had hoped. It was, in fact, very poor. There was still something lacking, and Ferguson needed to try to discover what it was. A chance phone call provided the answer.

Ferguson has often said that what happened as a result of that phone call, when Leeds contacted him to see if Man U would sell defender Denis Irwin, couldn't have been further from his mind. During the course of the conversation, Ferguson expressed an interest in Eric Cantona. Fergie had wanted another forward for some time, and, while the money was available, finding the right player was not quite so easy.

Leeds chairman Bill Fotherby said he would get back to him and did – very quickly. There had been problems at Leeds between Cantona and his manager, and some of the players were taking sides. The ill feeling could not be allowed to ferment in an otherwise happy and successful Leeds dressing-room and so Cantona was allowed to leave.

When he crossed the Pennines from Elland Road to Old Trafford, it was a very shrewd piece of business by Ferguson. The transfer fee was a bargain £1 million, and Cantona's performances against the Reds had shown the mark of an exceptional player. Many Manchester fans were taken aback by the news. They had no love for the Frenchman who had played so well against them. The Leeds fans were equally dismayed. The last place on the planet they would have wanted Eric Cantona to land was in the lap of Alex Ferguson and Manchester United.

The Frenchman proved to be the final piece in the jigsaw. It was not long before his influence was seen both on the training ground and in matches, and the cry of 'Ooh, aah, Cantona' was reverberating around the Theatre of Dreams. Players who thought they had been working hard in training were inspired to join Cantona for extra workouts. He practised and practised his skills, and the younger players followed his lead. They were not forced to, they were inspired to. His control of a game, his incisive passes, his individual ball control and his goal-scoring ability were outstanding. And as well as scoring goals himself, he proved to be one of the best playmakers seen in British football, providing numerous opportunities for his teammates to find the net. Even those who wanted to despise him found they had to grudgingly admit that he was something very special indeed.

Despite Cantona's extraordinary impact, there was nothing doing for United in the FA Cup, the League Cup or the UEFA Cup, but they stayed on course for the championship. Before their final home game of the season, Manchester United were acclaimed unassailable winners of the Premiership: it had become mathematically impossible for United to be caught. Ferguson was given the news when he was playing golf.

A few days later, United were at home to Blackburn Rovers, after which they were due to receive the league trophy. Rovers had to be beaten first, of course, otherwise the party would have been slightly spoiled. Fergie's men won 3–1, and club captain Bryan Robson and team captain Steve Bruce jointly lifted the trophy to the cheers and applause of the ecstatic Reds fans.

There were two men in the stadium that night who found it especially difficult to hold back the tears. One was Sir Matt Busby, who stood and applauded the new kings of Manchester. The other was Alex Ferguson. Both men knew what it was like to bring Manchester United out of the darkness and back into the spotlight, and I saw the emotion of it all get to them.

The nightmare was over; the dream had come true. Nobody was happier than Bryan Robson, who was, of course, one of the all-time

Manchester United greats. The adulation he received at West Brom as the manager who saved them from the drop at the end of the 2004–05 season matched anything he had heard at Old Trafford, but that special night when United lifted the trophy again was something that will no doubt live with him for ever.

At Old Trafford, Robson was acclaimed as 'Captain Marvel', while at The Hawthorns he was the former player who returned when things looked bad and proved to be the saviour who kept the team in the Premiership against all the odds. At West Brom, that was almost as good as winning a trophy.

Robson was born in Chester-le-Street, County Durham, on 11 January 1957 but began his football career some miles away with West Bromwich Albion in 1974. At the end of the 1974–75 season, he made his debut in a win over York City, little knowing that 30 years later he would be back at Albion in a totally different capacity. During the following 1975–76 season, Robson became a regular first-team player and earned a reputation for tremendous stamina, tough tackling, intelligent distribution and even getting in among the goals. He played a major part in West Brom's promotion back to the First Division, performing brilliantly whether he was used as a defender or in a more adventurous midfield role, and in 1979, he was made captain of the side.

By this time, he had already suffered more broken bones than most players sustain in a whole career, but he kept on coming back for more. His manager Ron Atkinson was impressed. 'You couldn't keep him down and who would want to?' said Atkinson. 'Whenever he was injured, he was totally focused on getting back into the side. I have never seen anyone recover from broken bones as quickly as he did. It was almost as if he was willing them to heal.'

International caps came his way, too. In February 1980, he made his full international debut in a European Championship qualifying match, a 2–0 victory over the Republic of Ireland. It was the first cap of many.

Robson became something of a hero to the West Bromwich supporters, and there was obvious disappointment when he joined Manchester United in 1981 for a then record transfer fee of £1.7 million. It was Ron Atkinson who persuaded him to join United. Atkinson had left West Bromwich to take over the managerial hot seat at Old Trafford and wanted his best player with him.

'What a fantastic player,' Ron said to me in a recent conversation. 'There have been few like him, and, certainly, at that time, he was quite unique. I don't think he would have left West Brom for any other club. He loved it there, but when he took a good look around Old Trafford, I think it made him realise what was on offer. He was the sort of player who was at his best on the big stage, and they don't come any bigger than Old Trafford.

'He was a great servant to the club while I was there, as he had been at West Brom, and the fact that he went on to become the longest-serving club captain of all time at Manchester United and also had such a brilliant England career speaks volumes.'

When Alex Ferguson arrived at Old Trafford, he was aware that the team captain was a very special player, but he did not realise that Robson was involved in the drinking culture that was causing some problems and possibly hampering the team's progress.

Make no mistake, Robson did not have a drink problem, but he liked to socialise with his teammates. Others would have seen their form suffer, but Robson was no ordinary player. His sheer hard work, both in training and during matches, seemed to offset any deteriorating effect the alcohol might have had on lesser mortals. But he was also prepared to listen to reason, and when Ferguson discussed the matter with him, Robson responded as a true pro, vowing to change his ways.

Ferguson has never had anything but praise to heap on his

former captain. 'He really was Captain Marvel with a real determination to win,' said Fergie. 'Robson was something very special. He gave everything he had every time, whether it was for us or for England. He had to not only win the game but to win every ball no matter whether it was a vital game or a practice match.

'Robson was a tremendous example to everyone else, and all the other players looked up to him. He was all you would expect of a captain and quite a bit more.'

When United won the Premiership for the first time, Robson was in the twilight of his playing days and planned to retire at the end of the following season. Injuries had been a problem for him throughout his career, probably because of his unflinching approach to the game. The ball was always to be won, no matter what the physical cost. Considering that he was out for some lengthy spells, it is even more of a wonder that he won 90 caps for England, scoring 26 goals. He also made 457 competitive club appearances for Manchester United.

During the 1992–93 season, Robson was in and out of the team as the newly signed Roy Keane made his presence felt in the squad and Paul Ince continued to impress. However, Captain Marvel did score his 99th goal for the club as United cantered to the Premiership title again and booked a place in the FA Cup final against Chelsea to try for the Double.

When Ferguson left Robson out of the side for the Wembley final, it was considered by many observers to be a heartless decision. However, Robson has never subscribed to that, even though it would have been his farewell performance for United and he might have turned those 99 goals into a milestone century. With Robson on the bench, Fergie's team won 4–0, apparently vindicating the manager's decision. Fergie has since said that he regretted not including Robson, at least as a sub. His decision at the time was purely tactical, but it would have been a nice touch to have given Robson the farewell he so richly deserved.

Robson left Manchester shortly afterwards, arriving at Middlesbrough in 1994 on a free transfer. He knew that as player–manager he had an exciting challenge to meet, a challenge that he met head on in his own inimitable style. With Robson at the helm, Middlesbrough won promotion to the Premiership in 1995 and signed such star players as Juninho and Fabrizio Ravanelli to help bolster a squad capable of taking on the best in the English game. It seemed that the club had made a big breakthrough in 1997 when they reached the finals of both the FA Cup and the League Cup, but, as so often happens, the team's league form left much to be desired and Middlesbrough were relegated.

Even that was not straightforward: Robson's side were deducted points for not fielding a team when illness struck the squad. Naturally, the club protested, but the FA held firm, and their action probably cost the side its place in the Premiership.

Pride was seriously damaged when Middlesbrough were relegated, both that of the club and of the manager. However, Robson's determination saw to it that the very next season, with him still in charge, Middlesbrough bounced back and were promoted to the top division once again, where they have remained ever since.

After a couple of mid-table finishes steadied the ship in the following seasons, a poor run of performances during the 2000–01 season threatened the club with relegation once again. Terry Venables was brought in on a consultancy basis in order to help Middlesbrough avoid the drop. Robson was understandably annoyed at having Terry Venables breeze in to hold his hand during the run-in to that season's finale. Although Robson had been one of the England team coaches under Venables and there were no personality problems between the two, the appointment still undermined Robson's status with the players and fans. If the club was relegated, it would all have been Robson's fault. If the club stayed up, it would be because Terry Venables had come to the rescue and single-handedly done the business. Bryan Robson was in a no-win situation.

Middlesbrough did manage to stay up, but Robson felt that his position was untenable and duly resigned. Like Fergie, Robson is his own man and to have someone brought in to watch over him was doubtless a blow to his self-esteem. Outer appearances suggested that Robson dealt with the situation calmly, but he must have been hurt by the club's apparent lack of faith. If the same had happened to Ferguson, it is doubtful whether he would have been so restrained.

It is a little ironic that when he left the Riverside Stadium at the end of that season, having played his part in the club's Premiership survival, his replacement was Steve McClaren. One former Manchester United man followed another, and Robson himself returned to Old Trafford to join the coaching team on a part-time basis. He mostly took charge of practice matches, and because his competitive streak was still so strong, he could not help but take part.

There was no way that Bryan Robson was going to be lost to football after he left Middlesbrough, but his appointment as the new manager of Bradford City in November 2003 was a surprise. It did not seem a likely career move, yet there was no doubt that he could offer the club a great deal. Although it was an unusual move, it was not without its merits, as it might just restore some of his self-esteem and remind people that he was still around. For Bradford, it was a great move, immediately increasing the profile of the club. However, when Robson joined a couple of months into the 2003–04 season, the team was already fighting relegation from the Premiership. Despite the difficulty of the task in hand, Robson remained optimistic. 'It was a challenge, but I felt good about the return to management,' said Robson at a press conference at the end of the season. 'I knew there was a good chance that the fight against relegation would not be successful, but I have never gone into something expecting to lose. It was a shame that we could not turn it round, but we didn't go down without a battle.'

Robson left Bradford during the summer of 2004, but it was only a matter of time before he would be asked back into management, although nobody could have guessed that his return to the game would be quite so dramatic. The call to arms came from West Bromwich Albion, a team very much in need of a lift. Gary Megson had done a fantastic job in taking them back to the Premiership but things were not working out, and it looked as if they were up to their armpits in the gaping hole of relegation.

It was a masterly move by the board at The Hawthorns, because Bryan Robson was still a folk hero at the club for whom he had once played. But his arrival did not make any immediate difference, and, in fact, he came in for a lot of criticism at first because results did not improve. There were even calls for the reinstatement of Gary Megson. However, Robson kept his head and gradually the team started playing in a more determined fashion. He organised things slightly differently, and even if the results did not change straight away, the performances certainly did. The feeling that the side was not going down without a fight restored faith among the supporters.

When the results did at last start to change, confidence increased even further, but it still seemed more like the spirited mindset of a condemned team rather than a genuine belief that staving off the inevitable was possible. Then came an incredible last day of the season and sheer delight when it became apparent that West Brom had indeed achieved the impossible and had avoided relegation. The players and fans went wild. And the manager? Well, from a man who had captained his country in World Cups and captained the most famous club in the world to trophies, came a simple statement. 'This is the greatest day of my life,' he said with a huge grin – and he meant it.

But how much did Sir Alex Ferguson play in that great West Brom escape? What Fergie lessons were brought to bear on that incredible push for survival? It would not be an exaggeration to suggest that the tactics and motivating skills Robson had learned from Fergie, coupled with his own determination, played a huge part in keeping the Baggies up.

'I learned a lot from him, but perhaps two of the greatest things were the kind of people he chose to have around him and his thoroughness,' said Robson. 'He is always very well organised in every department and leaves no stone unturned. Whether it is the treatment room, the kit hamper, pre-match meals, or whatever, there are no loose ends.

'He also likes his players to be mentally and physically strong. They have to be strong characters with determination and a will to win, to do well no matter what the circumstances. When I was at the club there were a lot of strong characters, and when you look at the signings he makes, you see that he goes for strength and mental toughness. Players coming into the club who do not have that will not last.

'He is the same with the coaching staff. He looks for men who have strength of personality and who are obviously among the best at their job. He likes to have people who are potentially managers themselves so that he knows that they not only have the coaching skills but also the ability to manage footballers and all their individual characteristics.

'He likes the whole set-up to be a proper team, and he will

openly discuss ideas with his coaches and assistants. He is approachable, too. If you want to know why he chose a particular player to operate in a different position for one match, he will tell you.'

Fergie's willingness to accommodate requests for help from those whom he respects is a part of his legacy to the game. There is no match for hearing it straight from the horse's mouth. It is Fergie's own continued enthusiasm for the game that makes him so willing to talk to those who show that same energetic drive and love of football as he does. He does not suffer fools gladly, but he will help anyone who has the common good of the game at heart.

'I think he sees it as a reflection on himself that people who have played for him or coached with him go on to have success as managers,' Robson added. 'He is always a big help and not only when you are there. He will always take your phone calls and give advice when it is asked. A lot of people have done and do that. I know I have.

'He is a positive thinker and has that same determination to succeed. It rubs off on everyone who works with him and perhaps that helped in giving West Brom the will to stay in the Premiership when all seemed lost.'

Robson spent nearly thirteen years at Old Trafford, eight of them working closely with Ferguson. Seeing Fergie in action from such a close vantage point on a day-to-day basis cannot fail to make an impression, as Robson explained: 'I don't think anyone could work with him as a player and not learn a great deal. As captain, I probably had more to talk to him about than most of the others, and while we had occasional differences of opinion, you could never say that he wasn't giving the club 100 per cent. You cannot fault that, and it is a great lesson for everyone in the game.'

Robson also noted that Ferguson was not just focused on football but on anything in which he took an interest: 'We shared a love of horse racing and Alex knew so much about the horses, the trainers, the owners, their favourite racecourses, everything. He was a mine of information and just as focused as in football. It is not surprising that his horse Rock of Gibraltar did so well since he had such a motivated boss.'

Bryan Robson has attempted to take that same thoroughness and determination into his own managerial career. While he is yet to emulate his former boss in terms of success, he undoubtedly demonstrates similar character traits and has evidently learned much from Ferguson. That is why he is one of the key beneficiaries of Fergie's football legacy. And what he has learned has also been of great benefit to the clubs Robson has managed, not least West Brom. Although the Baggies were relegated after the 2005–06 season, Robson will always be remembered for keeping them up when all seemed lost. It showed that he is a true survivor, just like his old boss.

7

SPREADING FERGIE'S GOSPEL

BRYAN ROBSON IS NOT THE ONLY MANCHESTER UNITED ALUMNUS TO HAVE BECOME a manager in the Premiership in recent years. Two of his equally inspirational teammates have also followed in their former boss's footsteps and taken on the responsibility of leading a top-flight football club. Welshman Mark Hughes and Englishman Steve Bruce worked under Fergie for many years and experienced both the highs and lows of playing for United in the late '80s and first half of the '90s. Both were leaders on the pitch and epitomised the strength of character and will to win that Ferguson looks for in his players. And both have had to call on that strength of character in recent times.

Although Mark Hughes is currently the manager of Blackburn Rovers, he first stepped into management in an unusual way by becoming player–manager of his country, proving himself to be the best Wales boss since Terry Yorath in the process. He gave his national squad self-belief and a determination to beat the best, even though they were considered to be the underdogs in almost every match. And since taking over at Ewood Park, he has shown that he is an astute young manager, guiding Blackburn to a top-six finish and a place in Europe in the 2005–06 season when many football pundits predicted they would be battling relegation. Without undermining the tremendous quality of the man himself, there is little doubt that this achievement is thanks in part to the time Hughes spent working with and observing Sir Alex Ferguson, something the younger man freely admits.

'I have played for many great managers, and I like to think I have learned something from each and every one of them,' Hughes said in a television interview. 'They are all so very different that I can honestly say that I have had a good football education.

'Having said all that, Sir Alex is such a dominant figure that you cannot go round him, and you cannot help but observe the way he does things. I must say that he has been a big influence on me and my career, and he has given me much advice which I try to put into practice.

'Managers need to have been able to study their previous bosses, and I took in a lot from observing Sir Alex. He has been brilliant for Manchester United and has won everything there is to win. If you cannot learn from him, from whom can you learn?'

Mark Hughes' football education began in Ruabon, which is not far from Wrexham in North Wales, where he was born on 1 November 1963. Rugby was the number one sport in Wales, but, fortunately, North Wales was influenced a little more than the rest of the country by Merseyside and Manchester, and football was popular. Hughes was especially influenced by Manchester United. 'I was a fan before I joined the club, and it was a big thrill for me to become a youth player there,' he said. 'To find yourself among players who you would normally be asking for an autograph took a little getting used to.'

Of course, it was not long before there were queues for Mark's autograph. He made his first-team debut on 30 November 1983 against Oxford, and it was the start of a senior career that was nothing less than brilliant. Mark is the only player to have won four FA Cup winner's medals and was twice voted PFA Player of the Year. Off the pitch, he was, and still is, quietly spoken and polite, but on the pitch, in the heat of a match, he was tenacious, totally committed to the cause and famed for acrobatic scoring which dazzled opponents and fans alike. His teammates were often dazzled, too, and some complained that he went for glory too often and should have distributed the ball more and quicker. But it's difficult to side with that argument when you look at what Hughes achieved in his career.

After helping United to win the FA Cup in 1985, Hughes was sold to Barcelona. Why he ever went remains unclear, but perhaps the lure of European football at a time when English clubs were banned from European competition was the reason. Hughes did not seem all that enthusiastic about the move, but the two clubs felt that they were both doing good business, Barcelona in adding another exciting player to their squad and Manchester United in adding £1.8 million to their coffers. The vested interests won the day, but both United and Hughes lost something when the contract was signed.

Ron Atkinson was well aware of this loss and was not keen to see his talented forward go. Atkinson knew that with Hughes in the side there was always the chance that something special would happen. 'Mark was always very lively,' he said. 'He did not play brilliantly in every single match, but his bad games you could count on your hands, and when he was in the team, you always knew you had a chance of grabbing those extra goals. He could be having a fairly quiet match by his standards, and then, suddenly, one half-chance and he would volley it into the net from any angle and sometimes from what seemed to be an impossible position. He wasn't just an excellent footballer and athlete but an acrobat as well.'

When Hughes got to Barcelona, he was out of sorts. He was not playing at the top of his form and did not settle in Spain. The presence of Gary Lineker, while being good for both men socially, was an added problem since they were largely in competition for the same first-team place. Terry Venables was in charge of Barcelona at the time and tended to favour Lineker.

Hughes was probably never more pleased to see someone than when Alex Ferguson, accompanied by Martin Edwards, visited him in Spain. The unsettled player wanted a return to Old Trafford, and United wanted him back. After some deliberations, Hughes' return to Manchester was arranged, and he witnessed the commitment of his new boss first hand. 'He was there to get me back to United, and I got the feeling that he would not leave until that mission was accomplished,' said Hughes. 'I was keen to come back, of course, but Alex talked to me as if he was having to sell the club to me, and his own belief and commitment to Manchester United was very impressive.

'I had been happy with Ron Atkinson as manager, but I knew that Alex Ferguson was going to be a very different kind of boss. He had a reputation for getting what he wanted, and he certainly impressed me when we met. I never changed my mind, and it was a great experience to be playing for him in a United shirt.'

His return to Old Trafford was not without complications: there were tax issues which had to be resolved and which meant that he needed to play elsewhere for a while. That somewhere else turned out to be Bayern Munich, and there is no doubt that their supporters would have liked Sparky to stay for much longer than the loan period that was arranged.

It cost £1.6 million to get Hughes back in his old United shirt, but it was certainly worth it as he played a major part in Fergie's revival plans and was inspired in the 1991 European Cup-Winners' Cup final against his former Spanish club, twice scoring to drive home the point that Barcelona had made a big mistake in not getting the best out of him when they had the chance. Hughes was extremely grateful that Ferguson had given him the opportunity and thankful that the fans were so accepting of him: 'I will always be grateful to Sir Alex for bringing me back from Spain and to the Manchester United fans for their understanding of me leaving and then returning to Old Trafford. It could not have been easy for them to just accept me back after I had previously left, but if they had any problem with that, they certainly didn't show it. They were brilliant to me, and they still are.'

Their willingness to welcome him back with open arms was in part due to the fact that Hughes was such a fantastic player and made such a massive contribution to United winning the Premiership title for the first time in 1993. He was also an integral part of the team that went on to win the Double the following season, scoring against Chelsea at Wembley to take an active part in the 4–0 FA Cup final victory. The fans had little to complain about!

It seemed that Hughes would be at Old Trafford for ever, but, of course, he wasn't. He finally left the club to join Chelsea in July 1995. The London outfit paid £1.5 million, but there was more to the deal than a simple sale transaction. The word on the street was that Fergie had wanted Hughes to go because he felt that the player had nothing more to offer. That was not at all the way it really was. In fact, Hughes had not put his signature to a proposed new contract that would have tied him to Manchester United for at least another three years. Also, if Ferguson had been so keen to sell Hughes, he would probably have done business with Everton, who had almost bought the player some months earlier.

Suggestions of animosity between Ferguson and Hughes are

largely unfounded, evidenced by the fact that when Mark Hughes was manager of Wales, Ferguson allowed Ryan Giggs to play in many more friendlies than he ever had previously. That is the sign of mutual respect, not the slap of non-cooperation.

Hughes played well for Chelsea and added a further FA Cup and Cup-Winners' Cup medal to his collection. He then played for Southampton, Everton and Blackburn Rovers before hanging up his playing boots in 2002 when he was 38. It was during these final playing years that he became manager of Wales. He did not hesitate to accept when he was offered the position: 'When I was asked to be manager of Wales, I could hardly refuse, because it is such a great honour, and I could not resist the challenge and the opportunity of putting my own thoughts into practice.'

Having played for his country many times and being a full-blooded Welshman, Hughes brought a passion to the job which had previously been lacking. Suddenly, Wales became a force to be reckoned with, and along with some great results, the national side also started drawing big crowds again.

However, making the transition from player to manager was not easy. 'When you are a player, you sometimes chat with the others about what you would do and what you would improve if you were the manager,' Hughes revealed at a press conference just after his appointment. 'I went from sitting among the players listening to and contributing to the usual criticisms of the manager, and the next minute I *was* the manager.

'I had to learn very quickly, having been thrown in at the deep end. You think on your feet in a situation like that, and I certainly drew on all the things I had observed from those managers I had worked for myself. I was learning minute by minute.

'One of the hardest obstacles to overcome is the change in your relationship with the players. You have to try to build on the relationship you have but change it so that the players who were tying their boots alongside you are comfortable with you now being the man who tells them what to do. You do not want to drive them away, just accept you as the same person in a different role.

'It is not easy for the new manager, and it is not easy for the players either. I think we overcame that with the Welsh team, but there are still players like Ryan Giggs who was my teammate both at club and country level, and you cannot just pretend that never happened.

'You really need a good rapport with the players, and I was lucky with Wales because we all wanted to do well, to turn it round, and that common cause worked for us. The players could have made it difficult for me, but they were brilliant and really responded.

'You have to be honest with them and let them see that you are your own man with your own ideas. There is no good in changing for the sake of change, but you do need to put your own stamp on things. That earns you the respect of the players and the will to do their best for you and for their team.'

With the respect of the players firmly established, the Wales side went on to achieve a run of results that was better than had been seen for many years. The team pushed for a place at Euro 2004, beating Italy at the Millennium Stadium along the way and eventually securing a play-off against Russia. A victory over the two legs would have seen them through to only their second major finals. However, it was not to be and Wales were eliminated. The despair of being so close yet so far was etched on the face of Mark Hughes on the night that his team so narrowly failed to qualify. It was a look that was reminiscent of Sir Alex Ferguson when his side have been knocked out of the Champions League. The two men may look nothing like each other but a yearning to win and passion for the game can be seen in both their faces.

It is not the only similarity between them, and Hughes has acknowledged that he has picked up some of the tactics that he witnessed Ferguson employ at Old Trafford. The most important of these is preparation: 'As well as the relationship with the players it is important to prepare well, and that was something Alex Ferguson always did. When I was playing, I used to think a lot about each game and how to prepare for it, and I think that has helped me a lot. There is no doubt that while I have never tried to copy any of the managers I worked for, I have picked up and used different elements from them all.'

With such giant strides having being made under Hughes, the Wales fans were extremely disappointed when their team manager accepted the job as boss of Blackburn Rovers in September 2004. He would have liked to have both taken the new job and kept the Wales one as well, but it was clear that he could not do that, so he reluctantly gave up his position with the national team.

Hughes' immediate target when he arrived at Ewood Park was the safety of Rovers, who were too close to the Premiership relegation zone for comfort at that time. He knew it was not going to be easy but a determination to succeed strengthened his will and that of his players, and in the final analysis, Rovers were safe. The supporters were ecstatic; Mark Hughes had not only been a hero at the club when he played for them but now he had saved them from relegation as well, and that made him a star twice over.

Hughes' stock rose even further in September 2005 when he took his Blackburn Rovers side to Old Trafford and won 2–1. He and Sir Alex shook hands after the game, and it was clear which was the happier manager. The new boss on the block had beaten the maestro, but Hughes was surprised by the negative chants that were directed towards Fergie from some of the United fans: 'It amazed me that when Blackburn won at Old Trafford back in September 2005, there were a few people at Old Trafford who actually booed him. Why? No manager can win every single game, and many managers would give their pensions to win as many matches and as much silverware as Fergie.'

Hughes has yet to win any trophies as a manager but takes inspiration from his former boss, whom he hopes to emulate one day. 'He is simply a marvellous manager,' Hughes said. 'How many managers have achieved European trophies with both a Scottish and an English club? Perhaps some people are not complimentary about his style, but there is no doubt that he gets results.

'He is a one-off – very special. He is at his most dangerous when he feels that he or his side has been coming in for some unjustified criticism. He creates a terrible backlash – woe betide the next team to play United after Fergie has been criticised!'

Hughes has been touted as a possible replacement for Sir Alex when the Scot finally hangs up his hairdryer (football speak for Fergie's habit of yelling in the face of his players New Zealand Maori style). Hughes rarely comments on speculation and would probably turn down the opportunity if it came along at the moment, as it is perhaps a bit too soon, but the memory of his spectacular bicycle-kick goals and his determined play in a United shirt means that there is little doubt that Sparky would be a popular choice with the fans.

Steve Bruce, on the other hand, would probably be a less welcome appointment, despite having also been mentioned as a possible successor to Ferguson in the past. While Hughes has seen his career blossom at Blackburn, Bruce has had a pretty torrid time of it of late, culminating in Birmingham's relegation to the Coca-Cola Championship at the end of the 2005–06 season. However, it was Bruce who won promotion for Birmingham in the first place, and he managed to secure mid-table finishes for the club in the preceding three seasons before they were relegated. He did this despite limited resources at Birmingham and a difficulty in attracting big-name players. And despite his recent disappointments, he has conducted himself with dignity, just as he did when he was Fergie's talismanic skipper.

But rather than gracing the turf of Old Trafford and captaining United, Bruce, one of Fergie's greatest ever signings, could have become a plumber instead. At the age of 17, he was about to start an apprenticeship at the local shipyard, thinking that his football chance had passed him by. 'I had trials with various clubs in the North-east and elsewhere, but it seemed that it was not going to happen for me,' Bruce told me in one of a number of interviews that I have conducted with him during his days at Old Trafford and since. 'I was offered an apprenticeship to do plumbing on ships being built in the Swan Hunter shipyard, and I was about to start when a call came from Gillingham offering me a place with them. Needless to say, I did not start my plumbing apprenticeship on the agreed date.'

Instead, Steve Bruce began learning his trade as a professional footballer. He was like a throwback to centre-halves of old: tough in the tackle, good in the air and totally fearless. 'No pain, no gain' could have been coined especially for Bruce, and his nose was broken time after time for the sake of his craft. It is a little ironic that when he was a boy he was considered to be talented but too small to stand up to the physical demands of football.

Bruce was born on 31 December 1959 and would have liked nothing better than to have played for Newcastle, his home-town side and the team he supported from the first time he took an interest in football. His father was a devoted Magpies fan and was delighted that Bruce followed in his footsteps.

He progressed through the ranks of the Newcastle Boys team and even played for the famous Wallsend Boys Club, which has produced many stars through the years. He had trials for teams near and far, including Burnley, Sunderland, Sheffield Wednesday,

Derby County, Bolton and, of course, Newcastle. It was after being rejected by them all that Bruce thought that he would have to find some sort of alternative career to football.

While playing in his last season with Wallsend Boys Club, Bruce travelled with the team to play in a tournament in Surrey. It was here that he was seen by Gillingham manager Gerry Summers and invited for a trial. Some hasty phone calls arranged for his apprenticeship at the shipyard to be put back, but it might as well have been cancelled altogether. The trial was a success and Steve Bruce became a professional footballer.

He developed as a player, bringing some prestige to Gillingham by gaining eight youth caps for England, and it became clear that he wasn't going to stay at the club for the rest of his career, no matter how far they progressed. Being a player from a lower-profile side who was winning youth caps for his country meant that the scouts were queuing up to watch him.

Norwich City signed him next, and he performed better than ever on the slightly larger stage. He relished each challenge and quickly gained a reputation for being an excellent young player. And the set-up at the East Anglian club made him feel right at home. 'Norwich City was very good for me,' he said. 'It has always been a very friendly club, not among the biggest but not a small club either. I had heard that Newcastle had wanted me before Norwich came in, and it would have been fantastic for me to go home to Newcastle, but it did not work out for one reason or another.

'Any disappointment I felt was quickly forgotten thanks to Norwich City, where Ken Brown was the manager with Mel Machin alongside him. They were a really good team, with people like Dave Watson and Chris Woods in the side. I still keep in touch with people at Norwich and have very happy memories of being there, especially as I made my second Wembley appearance with the Canaries.

'I had been at Wembley years before as a ball boy for the 1974 League Cup final but to play in the 1985 final not that long after joining the club from Gillingham was very special. We won 1–0, and it is hard to take in that you are really going up the steps to collect your medal. It is something that you have seen others do on television, but when you find yourself in that position, it is something that lives with you for ever.'

Steve was also named Man of the Match for a performance that not only impressed the football fans watching in the stadium and at home but also the directors, managers and scouts of many other clubs. One of those clubs was Manchester United, and when he was signed for £825,000 to play alongside Paul McGrath in the heart of the Reds' defence, a marriage made in football heaven began.

There was a hiccup at Bruce's medical, but one look at his playing record proved that he was made of stern stuff, and the deal went through. It was one of the best bits of business ever done by Ferguson: he did not just sign a useful defender, he signed a leader of men. 'Steve Bruce was a real bargain,' said Fergie. 'He was brave, talented and you could always rely on him. It was rare that he had a bad game. When he became captain, he led by example and gave everything for the club.'

While a Manchester United player, Steve Bruce won three Premiership titles ('93, '94 and '96), two FA Cups ('90 and '94), one League Cup ('92) and one European Cup-Winners' Cup ('91). Despite all these achievements, there was one major honour that eluded him. He never won the England cap that he so richly deserved. It is still a subject of some debate. 'It really is amazing that Steve never won an England cap,' said his United defence partner Gary Pallister, who was himself capped many times by England. 'He would not only have been great in the England defence but would also have been a brilliant captain. I suppose he was around at just the wrong time for his position, but it does seem strange that such a tremendous player was never honoured with a cap by his country.'

The disappointment of not receiving full international honours for England must have been even greater because he could have played for Northern Ireland, his mother being a native of Bangor. Those early youth caps for England sealed his international fate, otherwise he would surely have been capped by Northern Ireland many times and might even have been captain. That he was skipper of an England B team would have been scant consolation.

The leadership qualities that Bruce possessed, and which England missed out on, were most closely observed by Peter Schmeichel. The Danish keeper was a formidable last line of defence, but his job was made that much easier with Bruce in front of him. Despite working closely together on the pitch – or perhaps because they were so directly linked – they had the occasional disagreement. 'That is normal,' said Schmeichel. 'It is healthy to be passionate about the game and your team being on top. Yes, we used to shout at each other sometimes, but that was in the heat of the moment, and we were actually the best of friends and teammates. We were virtually neighbours, too. Any shouting was just for the moment and showed that we cared about what we were doing.

'I have had many defenders playing in front of me, and I don't think there were any better than Steve Bruce. He was an exceptional player and a very good captain. He would protect his teammates during a game and never flinched when the going was tough.'

Steve Bruce also had the reputation of being a thoroughly nice guy, good natured, ready to laugh and helpful to others. 'He was good in the dressing-room because he cared about the game but never got angry for nothing,' said Pallister. 'He had a sense of justice, but he was very rarely bad tempered. I can't think of anyone who would have anything but a good word to say about him, even the boss.'

Sir Alex had many good words to say about Steve Bruce but would still have an occasional rant at him. 'That's just the way he is,' said Bruce. 'He will have a real good go at everyone, and then it is all over. You just sit and keep your head down, and it blows over. It is not worth having a go back – it just prolongs the moment. You let him have his say, and if he is making a valid point, you remember it for next time. If he is just having a moan, you let him say his piece and then you get on with something else or go home. I always found it better to just listen and say very little.'

This pragmatism served him well and allowed him to work closely with Fergie during a period of considerable success. His sensible approach to dealing with his boss's outbursts meant that he was able to carry out the role of club captain for a number of years and was given the opportunity to lift some of football's greatest prizes. It also gave him the chance to become the first Englishman to captain a Double-winning side in the twentieth century when United won the league and cup in 1994. Despite being brought up as a Newcastle supporter, Bruce was devoted to the Reds and extremely proud when they did the Double.

'Although I was a huge Newcastle fan, I always considered Manchester United to be the biggest and the most famous club in the world,' said Bruce. 'When I joined the club and walked round Old Trafford for the first time as a United player, I felt that if nothing else ever happened to me in my career, I had made it to the top as a professional footballer. You don't get any higher than Manchester United.

'When we started to win things, it was like being in dreamland, and when I lifted the FA Cup knowing that we had done the

Double and it had been such a historic moment for both the club and me personally, it gave me a feeling that is beyond words.'

Of course, playing careers have to end some time, and Bruce began to work out what he would do in the future even before he retired. Like many other players, he had a few business interests, but he also knew he wanted to further his career in football – coaching or management seemed the obvious choice. Bruce had sampled some media work and had enjoyed it, but it was not what he really wanted to do for the rest of his life. He therefore undertook the necessary coaching courses with the real intention of one day repeating his playing success in the new role of manager.

First of all, though, there was still some playing to do, and Bruce joined Birmingham City in 1996 on a free transfer not realising that he would become manager at St Andrews a few years later. Ferguson was sorry to see him leave: 'It was a blow to lose Steve Bruce, because he had been such a great servant of the club. I was personally sorry to see him go, but he certainly took my respect with him.'

Bruce's first venture into the managerial hot seat was at Bramall Lane with Sheffield United, where he took over as player–manager in 1998. In 1999, he moved to Huddersfield and then to Wigan in 2001, soon followed by Crystal Palace later that year. Everywhere he went, he was well received by both the players and the supporters. The fact that he moved so often and so quickly during those years is certainly no reflection on his ability, it was simply as a consequence of a natural chain of events and the desire to compete at the highest level.

When he joined Crystal Palace, Bruce was perceived as a manager who would bring stability to a club which has a history of promotions and relegations. There was some controversy, therefore, when Birmingham City stepped in to make Bruce their manager not long after he had apparently committed himself to Palace. A row ensued between the two clubs, and it took some time before Bruce was actually able to take over as manager at St Andrews. In some small way it was similar to Fergie's own move from St Mirren many years earlier, a move that had also been clouded by controversy.

'I just wanted to get on with the job, so it was a frustrating time,' Bruce said. 'However, the best thing for me was to simply keep quiet and let the clubs sort it out between themselves. These things have a way of getting organised in the end, so I just waited, although possibly not as patiently as I should have, because I really wanted to get my teeth into the job.'

Eventually, of course, Bruce was able to do just that, and he steered Birmingham City into the Premiership in his first season with the club. He now found himself the manager of a top-flight side with relatively little experience behind him. It would be necessary to call on any help and advice that he could. Being just a phone call away from his former United boss, who rarely refuses advice to his former players, especially those who have earned his respect, was, therefore, extremely important. And Bruce also applied some of what he learned while at Fergie's side.

'As captain, I had to convey much of what the manager says to the players, especially during a game,' said Bruce. 'I think that gives you a greater insight into his thinking, and I was much more aware of his tactical thinking than many others.

'I think that you put things you have learned into practice without even thinking of where you learned them, but there must be quite a bit of influence on my own thinking from what I picked up while playing for him at United.

'He was always very shrewd and tactically very clever. The boss always knew as much as possible about the opposition, and, at times, he probably knew more about them than they knew themselves. He was a great exponent of how to prepare for a game, and I think that I learned much about that from him.'

All Fergie's former captains – such as Willie Miller, Bryan Robson and Roy Keane – know what it is to take the full force of his fury, but they also go onto the pitch knowing that they would not be captaining the side unless the boss felt they were capable. Bruce relished this extra responsibility and always accepted that more was expected from him as captain. 'He sets high standards for his captains,' said Bruce. 'That's fair enough. You are very limited in what you can do once a game has started. You have to have a team leader you can trust.'

Bruce also admired Ferguson's loyalty to his players and has adopted a similar approach. 'You never tell off any of your players in public unless they bring it upon themselves by their own conduct,' he said. 'Sir Alex never did that. He might shout and yell at you behind closed doors, but he did not blame his players for anything in public. Neither did he pick on any individual players for public comments, unless he felt there was something needed putting straight. I think that is an honourable way for a manager to conduct himself, and it earns the trust and respect of his players.'

Bruce has developed his own style of management and remains a nice guy, although he admits to the occasional rant in the dressing-room. He is no direct copy of Sir Alex Ferguson, but there are similarities, such as their desire for success and tactical approach to the game. Bruce has certainly instilled a never-say-die approach into his players. Had he not had so many of them sidelined by injuries, it is more likely that Birmingham would have stayed in the Premiership. As an ex-defender, Bruce favours defence, while as an ex-attacker, Fergie favours attack, but they both know that it is sometimes necessary to change tactics to suit the task in hand and also that it is necessary to keep their players motivated so that they compete until the last blast of the whistle. Bruce's face said it all when some of his players failed to respond.

There is no doubt that Bruce has had mixed fortunes at Birmingham, which remains a sleeping and possibly underfunded giant. Some managers thrive when they are constantly having to battle for survival – Dave Bassett or Harry Redknapp, for example. Others can only achieve their best when they are at a very big club with a big bank balance. Perhaps given the resources available to the manager of Manchester United, Bruce would be able to show what he can really do. And although he might not be an obvious candidate to replace Fergie at the moment, Bruce is no quitter and will do everything in his power to return Birmingham City to the Premiership. If he is successful, the United fans might once again talk about him as a future boss at the Theatre of Dreams.

8

AT FERGIE'S SIDE

BRYAN ROBSON, MARK HUGHES AND STEVE BRUCE WERE ALL THERE TO WITNESS THE turnaround in fortune that Fergie brought about at Old Trafford. Winning the Premiership in 1993, the first time the league had been won since 1967, was a special moment for the elder statesmen of the team, but the success did not end there. In fact, that league-championship victory marked the start of a decade of unprecedented success.

Following the return of the league trophy to Old Trafford, the next season promised more of the same. Manchester United were back in the driving seat of English football, and it was impossible to forget the words spoken by Alex Ferguson during his earlier days of crisis: 'We will get there, and when we do, life will change dramatically for Liverpool and the rest of football.'

During the summer, Roy Keane was bought from Nottingham Forest, and after some tough negotiation, Ferguson signed a new contract which would keep him at Old Trafford for some years to come. It seemed that Manchester United were set fair to take the title for the foreseeable future, a presumption that was underlined when they took the championship in the 1993–94 season with just four defeats in forty-two games. They reached the League Cup final, too, but came unstuck and lost 3–1 to Aston Villa, managed by, yes, you've guessed it, Ron Atkinson.

United also reached the final of the FA Cup. Chelsea were the opponents, and Eric Cantona took advantage of appearing on the most famous football stage in the world in front of millions of television viewers to give a performance that was well worth the 4–0 scoreline. He scored twice and controlled the game magnificently to help Mark Hughes and Brian McClair add their names to the FA Cup history book as the scorers of the other two goals.

Manchester United had done the Double and very nearly the Treble. However, their European campaign had ended early, and that was not good enough for Fergie or the fans, whose expectations had now been raised. The next step in the reawakening of United as a football force was success in the European Cup, and Ferguson would put increasing importance on that competition over the coming years.

However, participation in Europe is only guaranteed by strong performances in the domestic competitions and continued success in the league and cups was vital. But United did not win the championship every year, and the following season, Blackburn Rovers took the title. United were runners-up and reached the FA Cup final but were beaten 1–0 by Everton.

Fergie's side did not seem to have the same appetite as before. Perhaps that was due in part to the team changes which Ferguson was making or because some of the players felt that their days at Old Trafford were numbered. But it could also be that they were lacking the inspiration of Manchester's favourite Frenchman for much of the campaign.

The night of mayhem at Selhurst Park in January 1995 involving Eric Cantona was a combination of bad refereeing and players not listening to instructions. Crystal Palace were in their usual situation of having to fight a rearguard action against a superior Premiership side and must have known that they had precious little chance of stopping a rampant Manchester United, even on their own ground.

Instead, they chose to try to disrupt United's play and mix it in midfield, basically putting the visitors off their game. By half-time, United had more scrapes and bruises to show for their toil than goal chances. Alex Ferguson was a worried man. He knew his players would not be prepared to keep on taking physical aggression without retaliation. At half-time, he urged them not to get involved, but he also spoke to referee Alan Wilkie and suggested that he should be firmer.

Just four minutes into the second half, Ferguson had to watch helplessly as Palace's Richard Shaw pulled Cantona's shirt and scraped his leg once too often. The Frenchman lost his cool and lashed out. The referee brandished a red card, and Cantona was sent for an early bath. Then the real mayhem began when a supposed fan ran down the stadium steps to shout insults at Cantona as he left the pitch. United's French playmaker showed that he could kick more than footballs and launched himself at the offending supporter, who was by this time standing just behind the advertising hoardings that surround the pitch. Cantona's flying 'kung-fu' kick caught his verbal critic squarely in the ribs.

The attack was widely condemned, but, in truth, it earned Cantona many new admirers: many people thought that it was high time some mindless, foul-mouthed yob masquerading as a football fan was put in his place. Unfortunately, the football authorities were not quite so understanding and promptly threw Cantona out of the game for nine months. He was also sentenced to 120 hours of community service by a criminal court. United's manager could do nothing but stand by and watch as his team's season was effectively ended there and then.

After the loss of the Premiership title, the sale of Paul Ince at the end of the 1994–95 season prompted further questions about Ferguson's management skills. He stated that it was his choice to sell the midfielder because he felt that Ince's attitude was wrong and there was an apparent lack of enthusiasm by the player to change it. Ince claimed that he was being forced out of the club, and most of the fans preferred to listen to their playing hero rather than the boss. Despite winning back-to-back championships and the Double, Ferguson had still not earned the supporters' full loyalty.

However, at the end of the 1995–96 season, Fergie's credentials were once again confirmed as United did the Double for the second time in three seasons. And the following year, the Reds were crowned champions again, but the annual exit from the now European Champions League was beginning to grate on the manager. True, performances were improving but there was annual disappointment.

Nobody could have guessed what drama was ahead. United won the title again in 1999 – after losing out to Arsenal in 1998 – and booked a place in the FA Cup final thanks in part to a wonder goal by Ryan Giggs in the semi-final. Meanwhile, there were some tremendous displays by United in the European Champions League which saw them into the semi-final against Juventus.

Alex Ferguson described the second leg of that tie as 'the greatest performance ever produced by a team under my management'. A 0–0 draw at Old Trafford in the first leg put the ball firmly in the court of the Italians, and when they took a 2–0 lead at the Stadio delle Alpi, it seemed as though United would once again be forced to watch the final as spectators. However,

Roy Keane scored and Dwight Yorke put United level, and it looked as if United might just squeeze through on the away goals rule. Then Andy Cole made it 3–2, and there was no way back for the Italians – United were through to the final.

Newcastle were beaten in the FA Cup final, and the Double was secured, but there was no time for celebrations. The team had to fly to Spain for the climax of the season: the European Champions League final against Bayern Munich at the Nou Camp.

No words could do justice to the drama of the final itself, but, needless to say, Ferguson had a huge influence on how the evening's events unfolded. Substitutions are one of the few tools that a manager has at his disposal to change the outcome of a match once it has kicked off, and Ferguson has acknowledged the importance of making the right replacements at the right time: 'Substitutions are always a big decision. They can win you a game, or even lose you one, and managers can be villains or heroes depending upon whom they take off, who they put on, when they do it and what the final score is.'

His substitutions that night proved to be invaluable. He brought on Teddy Sheringham for Jesper Blomqvist in the 67th minute and Ole Gunnar Solskjær for Andy Cole in the 81st. Their contribution was to be immense.

There are still those who claim that Manchester United were fortunate winners, but Bayern did not really deserve anything more than they got. They scored after six minutes and thought that was the end of the game. They believed that they could defend their slim lead for the next 84 minutes and settled in to keep the Reds out.

In contrast, United tried everything to break down their resolute opponents but just couldn't seem to get the ball into the net. Dwight Yorke and Andy Cole, who had been such a deadly duo all season, ran up against a brick wall and ran out of ideas.

At half-time, Ferguson spoke kindly to his players. He told them that they had worked hard and did not deserve to be a goal down. He said that if they kept up the same pressure, the Germans would crack. He also told them that if they lost, they would remember it for the rest of their lives.

Ferguson could not fault his team's effort in the second half, but the players were still not breaking down the tough Bayern defence. A further throw of the dice was required and the manager made his substitutions, knowing full well that it was make-or-break time. With Sheringham and Solskjær on the pitch, United threw everything at the Germans, who were exhausted but determined to hold their ground. The ninety minutes ticked away, and the fourth official announced three minutes of extra time.

United gained a corner and everyone rushed forward, including a giant wearing a different coloured jersey to his teammates in red. Peter Schmeichel, the world's best goalkeeper, playing his last game for Manchester United, decided to turn himself into a centre-forward. While the Bayern players worked out who would mark Schmeichel, David Beckham swung in a deadly corner. Confusion reigned, a foot connected with the ball and it ran into the net. The golden boot of Teddy Sheringham had struck.

For a brief moment, there was silence: shock was etched on the faces of the Germans, and even the United players did not seem to realise at first the full implication of that ball crossing the white line. Suddenly, the place erupted; United were back in the game. Extra time was on the cards, and Manchester had been given a lifeline.

The game restarted, Bayern lost possession and the United charge was on again. Another corner was won, and another dangerous cross was put into the box. Again, it was Sheringham who reacted first, nodding the ball on, and Solskjær was there to boot the ball into the roof of the net.

A number of the German players collapsed, some of them in tears. The United fans in the stadium were delirious, and the referee harried the players to get the game restarted. He blew his whistle, and the ball was in play again – for just 15 seconds. The next time he whistled, it was to signal the end of the match. It was all over, and the manager's 'supersubs' had scored a goal apiece to give Manchester United the European Cup for the first time since 1968.

Anyone who still felt that Fergie was not the right man for the job was finally silenced. What price Alex Ferguson now? Or should that be what price Sir Alex Ferguson now, since the Queen's Birthday Honours list was amended at the 11th hour to include the Manchester United manager, who followed in the footsteps of Sir Matt Busby and Sir Bobby Charlton when he was knighted.

Where do you go after you have won the biggest prize in European football and all there is to offer on the domestic scene? There are two options. You either rest on your laurels, having done it all, or you try to do it all again. Fergie was more inclined to do the latter, and it was not long before he was making further adjustments to his team and trying once again to win everything that was going.

Since that unforgettable night in Barcelona, the trophies have continued to be collected, although there has been no further joy in Europe, and even with Ruud van Nistelrooy leading the goal charge, there has not been a return to the excellence and supreme success of the '90s. In fairness, there have been few seasons when Fergie's men have not collected some sort of silverware, and he has a bigger personal trophy haul than most football clubs. After winning the European Champions league, United won the Premiership for the next two seasons. Arsenal intervened during the 2001–02 season, but United bounced back to retrieve the trophy at the end of the 2002–03 season. The FA Cup was also won again in 2003–04. The 2004–05 season was barren, although it was conceded, albeit grudgingly by some, that Arsenal's defeat of Manchester United in the FA Cup final was an injustice.

During this time, new players arrived and others went. Some played well but many others were disappointing. David Beckham left United for Real Madrid under something of a cloud, and Diego Forlán promised much but never actually delivered, rather like Jordi Cruyff, Juan Sebastián Verón and, of course, French international goalkeeper Fabien Barthez, who proved to be more of a liability than a confidence-boosting custodian.

It is not that these were bad signings, as such. On paper, the signing of Barthez should have been a masterstroke. Peter Schmeichel left a huge gap when he left, and the problem of filling his boots was immense. Logically, replacing the Danish international with the French international who had World Cup and European Championship winner's medals to his credit, should have been the perfect answer. But nobody could have predicted the erratic displays that Barthez would give, any more than they could predict that any top-flight player joining the most famous football club in the world would fail to give of their very best.

There have also been controversial moments, such as the time United opted out of the FA Cup so that they could take part in the new World Club Championship. Ferguson was in two minds about that decision, but it was not taken exclusively by him. And there was the famous dressing-room row with David Beckham.

It remains unclear exactly what happened that day, but there are two main theories: the official story that was released to the press and the conspiracy theory that was circulated by the gossipmongers. The official story is that Ferguson was so angry after a game against Arsenal that he kicked a boot which was lying on the dressing-room floor and it accidentally struck Beckham above the eye. The conspiracy theory states that Ferguson was so angry with Beckham that he deliberately kicked the boot at him. However, if Fergie had intentionally aimed the boot at Beckham, it would have been such a feat of skill and accuracy that the boss could easily have replaced Beckham and taken the team's free-kicks himself. As Fergie himself said, 'If I tried it a hundred or even a million times, it could not happen again. It was a freak accident, and he needed no stitches. The club doctor dealt with it, and there was nothing more to be said. We move on.' Fergie also played down the gravity of the injury: 'It was just a graze.'

But an anonymous member of the Beckham camp, fanning the flames of intrigue and controversy, claimed that the injury was much more serious: 'There was blood still dripping from it two hours afterwards.'

It seems extremely unlikely that this was the case, and surely the club doctor or physio would have become more involved if Beckham had been dripping blood for a couple of hours after the incident. However, it was obvious that some kind of contact took place, so there was little sense in a manager denying the incident had taken place.

The truth of the matter will probably never be known. Fergie's rages are not uncommon and most players tend to look at the floor or divert their attention at such times, so there are likely to be fewer witnesses to the 'flying boot' incident than might be expected. However, the likelihood is that it was just an accident. It would be difficult to imagine a situation in which a manager would wish to damage one of his own players, even in the heat of the moment. Beckham later drew a line under the incident by saying there was harmony in the dressing-room, but, at the time, the newspapers delightedly turned the spotlight on the disharmony between two of the biggest names in football.

There have, of course, been other controversies involving Fergie in recent years: there was the great wrangle over Ferguson's racehorse, Rock of Gibraltar, and its stud rights; the takeover of United by the Glazer family; the retirement U-turn; the war of words with Arsenal's Arsène Wenger and Chelsea's José Mourinho; and his continued support of New Labour. In fact, controversy has followed Ferguson throughout his career, and he has rarely been out of the news since he began his days as a player. But he has always risen above contentious debates, and his ability to deal with such difficult challenges has only strengthened his position as a man to emulate. He has the kind of experience that money simply cannot buy.

It is those people who have worked directly alongside him that have probably had the best access to this pool of knowledge. In particular, the lucky few who have had the opportunity to work as his right-hand man have been in a unique position to benefit from his expertise.

Fergie's assistants have been a varied bunch. Archie Knox, whom Ferguson worked alongside for many years, has always been the kind of man who likes to keep in the background, and he has remained an assistant for the majority of his career. However, other assistants have used the platform of working with Ferguson to create a name for themselves on the way to their own managerial positions. Some have been unheard of before their association with Ferguson and Old Trafford, whereas others have already been famous in their own right. Brian Kidd was one of those who was a hero even before Fergie arrived on the scene.

Kidd was almost destined to become involved with Manchester United. He was born in Manchester and supported United from a very early age. 'I don't remember when I started supporting United, but I was a huge fan,' he told me in an interview some years ago. 'I think it was a family thing. I do remember that whenever anyone asked me what I wanted to do when I grew up, I always said I wanted to be a footballer and play for United. It was my dream, and it came true.'

There were family celebrations when he signed preliminary forms for United at the age of 14, and, of course, he was the envy of his schoolmates. Less than a year later, he signed apprentice forms and did the usual boot cleaning while learning his trade at the famous United youth-training scheme. And his progress through the ranks continued when he was taken on full time. 'I was offered a full professional contract when I was 18 and signed without hesitating,' Kidd said. 'I still could not believe that all this was happening. It was fantastic. But it just got better and better. Matt Busby was manager at the time, and he was a tremendous manager to work for. He was especially good with young players and always made you feel that you were as important to the club as any of the established first-team stars.

'He was a very patient man with a kind personality. That does not mean that he would not get angry at times and tell people off, but he was always fair, and if you did get on the wrong end of his annoyance, you felt really bad about it, because you just didn't want to offend such a nice guy.'

Kidd made his first-team debut on 19 August 1967 in an away match against Everton. Any thoughts that it might have just been a run-out to see how he would perform were quickly dispelled when Busby made it clear that Brian Kidd was now a regular first-team player. He played in all but four games for the United first team that season, but the highlight came at the end of the campaign.

'It was my 19th birthday when we played Benfica in the European Cup final at Wembley, and what a night that was. I was thrilled when we got there, because I had played a part in our reaching the final. The night itself was one of those occasions that will always be vivid in my memory.'

Kidd had scored an all-important goal in the third round of the competition against Górnik Zabrze. In the first leg, United were leading 1–0 with a minute to go when Brian Kidd backheeled a pass from Jimmy Ryan and ensured that United took a two-goal cushion to the return match in Poland. They lost 1–0 in the second leg, and Kidd's goal proved to be the tie winner.

United then progressed through the competition until they reached the semi-final against Real Madrid. It proved to be a real heart-stopper of a tie. George Best scored a stunning goal to make it 1–0 in the first leg at Old Trafford, and the second leg was full of drama as Madrid took a 3–2 aggregate lead at half-time, only for Munich survivor Bill Foulkes to score in the second half and send United into the final against Benfica.

'So there I was as a young man with both my birthday and the biggest game of my life on the same day,' Kidd recalled. 'It was an amazing day at Wembley. Matt made sure that everyone kept their nerves under control. He kept talking to us individually and as a squad and kept us in high spirits throughout the day. Then, as the game approached and we arrived at Wembley, he pointed out how much it would mean to the club and to him personally to win the trophy and also how much it would mean to the supporters. We drove through thousands of them as our coach reached the stadium, and when we walked out for the match, there were so many United scarves it was almost like a home match.

'It was exciting and nervy, but we just had to keep our heads. We knew that we could hardly have had more difficult opponents than Benfica with Eusébio in their line up. We were confident, though, and for the spectators, it was a classic game with the bonus of extra time.

'The boss was great during the break before the start of extra time. He just quietly told us that we were doing well and we now had the chance to finish the job and take the trophy, because Benfica were visibly tired. It only needed a little more effort from us and they would crack.

'He was absolutely right. Bestie scored a brilliant goal soon after the restart, and a couple of minutes later, a cross came over and it was perfect for me to head into the net. When Bobby Charlton blasted in his second goal, and our fourth of the night, we knew we had only to keep possession for the remainder of the match.

'It was a very emotional moment when the whistle blew and Matt ran on to the pitch to greet us, especially for Bobby and Bill Foulkes, who, with him, had survived Munich. It had been a victory for the club and the fans but also for the memory of those who had not survived the plane crash. For me, it was an incredible 19th birthday.'

Brian Kidd's career blossomed from there. He became a full England player just before his 21st birthday, playing against Ecuador on his debut. Things were going well for him, but he wanted to broaden his horizons. 'Although I was a United man at heart, I wanted to gather more experience than playing for just one club, so I joined Arsenal in 1974 and stayed at Highbury for two years before moving back to Manchester for a short spell with City and then on to Everton and Bolton. I also played in the United States for four years before I decided it was time to come home and get involved with coaching and management.

'Playing had been a great experience, and I had already learned a lot from Sir Matt and the other managers for whom I had played. When I decided to go into management in 1984, it was like starting a new career, although I had lots of ideas and the knowledge I had gained from watching the managers and coaches when I was a player.'

Little did Brian Kidd know then that his education was only just beginning. After largely unspectacular periods as boss of both Barrow and Preston, it seemed that management was perhaps a bigger stride than he was ready for at that stage in his career. All was not lost, though, as he was soon to enrol in the Alex Ferguson (unofficial) school of football management.

In 1988, Brian Kidd was appointed youth coach at Old Trafford. His brief was to find and nurture the young talent of Manchester and the surrounding areas to keep the United youth-team conveyor belt churning out new stars. 'It had been noticed that Manchester City was getting some really good youngsters, and we wanted them for ourselves,' said Kidd. 'My job was to get them and coach them on the way to becoming potential first-team players with United.'

Kidd's mission was successful, and one of his first recruits was Ryan Giggs: 'I heard about him from one of the stewards, went along to see him and realised that I was seeing something a bit special. The snag was that he was already training with Manchester City. Alex went round to his house after he played in a trial match for us. He talked to him and his mother for a while and offered him terms, and Ryan signed. City had failed to actually sign him, so we were delighted when he joined us.'

When Archie Knox left the club in 1991, Ferguson needed a new assistant. It took him four months to decide who it was going to be, but in August of that year, Brian Kidd became his new right-hand man.

'It was very flattering to be asked, and I was really up for it in many ways,' said Kidd. 'The only problem I had was that I did not really want to leave the youth squad, because we had some really promising players coming through, and I felt that I had not completed the job.

'Having said that, the opportunity to work alongside Alex was too good to turn down, so I decided to go for it. I have never regretted that decision. It was good to see some of those young players make it to the United first team and then go on to play for their countries and, in some cases, attain football stardom.

'It was also good to work alongside the boss and learn from his methods. I did not agree with everything he did or said, and we did have our moments of serious disagreement, but, by and large, we got on OK and had the common cause of taking United to the Premiership title and beyond.'

It is common knowledge that Fergie and Kidd had some huge arguments, but, then, Fergie has fallen out with many people. His determination to get his own way makes him difficult to work with. The trouble is that he is so often proved to be right. However, their relationship was far from being one long battle. They shared many great moments and were both determined that United should make success a habit.

They did exactly that, of course, beginning with the Premiership victory in 1993. When Steve Bruce scored to make it 2–1 at home to Sheffield Wednesday at the end of that campaign, and effectively win the title for United – although mathematically it was still not theirs – Kidd and Ferguson famously hugged each other and danced about together on the pitch at Old Trafford. It was one of those mad moments that happens in football and is always remembered. Alex Ferguson had never seemed like the sort of guy who would hug anyone, let alone a member of his staff. He and Brian Kidd were chalk and cheese, but somehow their talents had combined to create a Manchester United side that was possibly even better than the team which had earned so much acclaim in the '60s. And it was apt that Brian Kidd was so closely involved in that 1993 title triumph because he had also been there the last time United had won the championship 25 years earlier.

In the years that followed, the combination of Alex Ferguson and Brian Kidd seemed unbeatable. The Premiership and FA Cup

Double followed in 1994, a feat which was repeated in 1996. The European Champions League was the next big trophy in their sights.

Out on the street, it was sometimes said that Kidd had brought something that Archie Knox could never have contributed. It was even suggested that Kidd was really the power behind the throne. But it was a shock to Fergie when his assistant announced that he was leaving in December 1998. United were in the hunt for the championship and European glory at that time and were looking very good indeed. However, Brian Kidd had his own ambitions and revealed that he wanted a crack at management again. Blackburn Rovers were looking for a replacement for Roy Hodgson, and Kidd was duly appointed.

Kidd had previously been linked with Everton but had been persuaded to stay at Old Trafford. This time, there was no stopping him. Ferguson questioned whether Kidd was ready for management but that probably only made him all the more determined to try. His departure was swift and left a gap alongside Ferguson, who admitted that Kidd would be missed because he had such a good rapport with the players.

Kidd then faced the daunting task of turning round the fortunes of Blackburn Rovers. It was not a marriage made in heaven, and Kidd left Rovers without making much impression, returning to coach Leeds United when David O'Leary was in charge. Perhaps the difference between coaching and management was a bridge too far for Kidd. He would not be the first excellent coach to find it difficult to make the transition to manager and the numerous rigours of that job.

There has been talk of Kidd returning to Old Trafford to work once again with Ferguson in a youth-coaching role, but there has also been much talk of rifts between the two men, so the chances of them getting together in any capacity seem quite remote. Brian

Kidd has his pride, and Sir Alex Ferguson can be extremely stubborn.

But what went wrong in their relationship? Any attempt to answer that question would be speculative, but rumours have circulated and various theories have been put forward. For example, Kidd has been accused of moaning behind Ferguson's back about coaching methods and tactics. It is alleged that he complained to directors and just about anyone who would listen. Another theory is that Ferguson did not like Kidd's popularity, both among the fans and among the players, and it has been argued that Ferguson saw Kidd as some kind of threat to his exalted position. It has also been said that while they performed well together professionally, their personalities clashed outside of work. Ferguson has a reputation for being verbally abrasive and hard to communicate with, whereas Kidd is known to be quite relaxed and approachable, only losing his temper when there is a very good reason for it. There is also a chance that Kidd thought he deserved a little more recognition for the young players he found and nurtured breaking into the first team and becoming international stars. Ferguson may have interpreted this as Kidd having ideas above his station.

Ultimately, however, all this adds up to is conjecture, and the real test of their relationship is the success Manchester United enjoyed on the pitch. The evidence is there for all to see that the two men formed a partnership that had the rest of the Premiership trailing in their wake. And Kidd has also made it clear that he enjoyed working with Ferguson as well as finding it an educational experience. 'I loved the job and being at Manchester United, and I include in that the aspect of working with Alex,' said Kidd. 'He and I often did not share the same opinion, and we would have our disagreements. Having said that, I certainly enjoyed working with him, and I have fond memories of the success we had and how it was achieved. It was a great experience, and I can certainly call upon that time and the things learned as I go about my coaching work now.'

Although Kidd has been taking a break from football since being diagnosed with cancer in 1994, it would not be beyond the realms of possibility that he might one day return to the club that has been such a big part of his life. People whose lives have been touched by an institution such as Manchester United often find themselves drifting in and out of it. Old Trafford is like a magnet that will pull those who have experienced its magic back from just about anywhere else on the planet. Perhaps Kidd will return in a post-Fergie period, and if it does one day happen, Manchester United will benefit from the legacy that Ferguson is amassing in more ways than one.

9

McCLAREN CALL

IN THE SUMMER OF 1998, AFTER A RARE SEASON WITH NO SILVERWARE, FERGUSON found himself without an official assistant. Brian Kidd's management ambitions had led him to join Blackburn Rovers and a replacement had to be found. It took several months, but, eventually, Steve McClaren was prised from Derby County, where he was assistant to Jim Smith.

McClaren was a surprise appointment, and most United fans at the time asked, 'Steve Who?' Being the first-team coach at Derby County was not the most high-profile job, and Fergie's new assistant was not someone that most people had heard of. In fact, even Martin Edwards, then chairman of United, wasn't sure exactly who had been appointed, announcing that 'Steve McClaridge' had been chosen to work alongside Fergie.

Although McClaren might not have been an instantly recognisable name, his coaching abilities were certainly known to the United boss, who had recognised a rare talent. Fergie's new assistant was a progressive young coach who had all the relevant badges and qualifications. This made him a very different character to his new boss, who had learned how to be a coach and manager by doing rather than studying. After the apparent personality clashes with Kidd, it might have been expected that Ferguson would appoint a like-minded assistant. However, the United boss has always put success on the pitch before personal relationships and realised that McClaren could bring something extra to the side.

Fergie has always been able to spot talent, whether it be a player or a coach, but even he could not have foreseen McClaren's meteoric rise to the position of England manager. After a convoluted process that drew criticism from many observers, McClaren was announced as the successor to Sven-Göran Eriksson on 4 May 2006. When asked to comment about McClaren's appointment, Ferguson made it clear that he was confident that the FA had appointed the right man for the job: 'I think it is a good appointment. He knows the England players and has had a good apprenticeship.'

Part of that apprenticeship, of course, had been served under Fergie at Manchester United. The importance of this time spent working with the United boss cannot be underestimated. If McClaren had not been exposed to the highest levels of football when working for Ferguson, it is unlikely that he would have been considered suitable for the position. One of the criticisms of the British candidates for the England job – who were widely believed to be Alan Curbishley, Sam Allardyce and Martin O'Neill – was that none had experienced what it was like to win the really big prizes that football has to offer. Alan Hansen highlighted this problem in his column for the BBC website:

> What England want in an ideal world is a manager that has
> been competing in the Champions League, who has been

winning the Premiership. But unfortunately, those managers are all foreigners. It is a sort of catch-22 situation. People talk about England managers having big-time experience, but that will only happen if the big clubs take a chance on them.

Although Middlesbrough are not considered to be a big club, McClaren had witnessed first hand what it was like to win the Champions League and Premiership, having been directly involved in bringing success to United when he was Fergie's assistant. This gave him an edge over his competitors.

He also had the advantage of having been part of the England set-up already. McClaren had worked for the national side, on and off, since 2000 and had been groomed to take over one day. Ferguson recognised the importance of this continuity. 'England have a good set of players, an experienced back-room staff and Steve knows all that,' said the Scot. 'Steve has a knowledge of the staff and of the players, so I hope he does well, because it's not an easy job.'

It was a point that was not lost on Brian Barwick, chief executive of the FA. He had been forced into an extremely embarrassing position when he had initially offered the job to the current Portugal and ex-Brazil manager Luiz Felipe Scolari, only for the Brazilian to turn him down. Barwick had courted 'Big Phil' in the first place because he also recognised that most of the leading English candidates were perceived to be too inexperienced. But McClaren was the exception, and Barwick emphasised the pedigree of the new England manager at the press conference to announce his appointment. 'He has an excellent reputation in the game,' said Barwick. 'He's been involved in big matches, has worked alongside footballers with big reputations, has experienced big competitions and this is now his big opportunity. He has been involved in major international and top-class football in his roles alongside Sven, for England, and Sir Alex Ferguson, for Manchester United.'

McClaren's pleasure at being offered the chance to become the manager of England was obvious when it was his turn to speak at the press conference. 'This is the biggest honour that any coach can have and is obviously the highlight of my career,' he said. 'It's a massive challenge and one that I welcome. I have hugely enjoyed my time at Middlesbrough and am very grateful to the club. However, this was an opportunity I couldn't refuse, and I'm probably the proudest man in England today.'

McClaren was unable to suppress his smile, perhaps because even he realised that his rise as a coach and manager had been nothing short of astonishing, especially as his playing days were less than impressive. He was born in York on 3 May 1961 and had pursued a career in football from an early age. He never really considered doing anything else and gradually made the grade through schools football to be offered a place with Hull City in 1979.

As a midfielder he developed an understanding of the game beyond his years, but he did not have the playing talent to become a star. However, he played 178 times for Hull City's first team before leaving in 1985 to join Derby County. His finest hour was in 1987 when he helped Derby win the then Second Division title. 'It was a great moment for me,' he recalled. 'You find that there are some top players who consistently win medals and caps, but for the majority, those are rare achievements. For someone like me, winning the Second Division was worth celebrating.'

The celebrations did not last long, however, as Derby brought in some fresh blood for their First Division campaign, and McClaren found himself struggling to get into the first team. He had a brief loan spell with Lincoln City before agreeing to a permanent move to Bristol City. 'It was a difficult decision in some ways, because I didn't want to give up on fighting for a place with Derby, but, on the other hand, I wanted regular first-team football and that was on offer at Bristol City,' said McClaren.

In 1989, he moved again, this time to Oxford United, where midfield was a problem position for the club. It was thought that his experience and ability could make a big difference. Sadly, a persistent back injury sidelined him at Oxford and eventually ended his playing career at the age of 27 when many midfielders are just coming into their own, their experience giving them a much greater command of the game.

'I didn't want to quit football at all, and there was a chance to become a coach, so that suited me fine,' said McClaren. 'At that stage, I never thought about being a manager one day, but coaching interested me, and if that was going to be my new career, I wanted to really go into it properly.'

McClaren proved to be a natural coach, but he also ensured that he gained all the necessary qualifications as well, attending the courses stipulated by UEFA. However, waving a certificate to prove that you have passed a course is not all it takes to be a really successful football manager. You also have to be able to relate to your players, something that came easily to McClaren from the beginning. No doubt this contributed to him being appointed as Oxford's youth-team coach. It was a role that McClaren enjoyed: 'Coaching youth football is great because you see so much raw talent, and you can help these guys with their careers simply by improving their individual skills and developing their understanding of the running of the game.'

He did not stay in charge of the youth team for long, though, as he was promoted to the position of reserve-team and then first-team coach. McClaren was getting the kind of results that made others in the game start to sit up and take notice.

Jim Smith, one of the most respected coaches and managers in the game, recognised that Steve McClaren had something to offer and took him back to Derby County in 1995 as his right-hand man. 'He was his own man, and he thought about innovative coaching and tactics,' said Smith. 'He had the reputation of being easy to work with and of being dedicated to his job and to the club and its players. I wanted someone like that as my number two at Derby County.'

Smith got his man, but it cost Derby £30,000 to compensate Oxford for the loss of their bright young coach and potential manager. But it was still a great move for all concerned: Oxford were able to use the money wisely, and McClaren was able to return to the Baseball Ground and introduce some fresh ideas at Derby County. Jim Smith was now confident that he had both the playing staff and coaching team to make a serious attempt at winning the First Division championship and a place in the Premiership.

The combination of Smith and McClaren worked wonders for Derby County, and at the end of his first season with the club, McClaren was celebrating again, the club having won the First Division title and a coveted place among English football's elite. 'It was like history repeating itself,' he said. 'When I joined Derby County as a player, we won the Second Division title, and now as a coach back there, we did it again. The name of the division had changed from Second to First, but the end result was the same.'

Derby County gave a reasonable account of themselves in the Premiership, hovering in the mid-table safety zone and pulling off enough surprise results to keep the fans happy. Even though Jim Smith's reputation and track record spoke for itself, much of the team's success was attributed to Steve McClaren, whose reputation as an outstanding coach was growing. He was certainly mentioned to Alex Ferguson when he was seeking someone to replace Brian

Kidd as his assistant at Manchester United. Scouts and other contacts presented Fergie with a hit-list of possible coaches to become his number two, and McClaren was appointed early in 1999.

Jim Smith was less than happy as he told me later when discussing the Derby days: 'I was not pleased to lose Steve. There is no way I would stand in his way, though. You just don't do that. He had a talent that needed to be expressed, and I was pleased for him that it had been recognised outside of Derby County.'

Recognition of McClaren's talents only increased at Old Trafford as the new coach presided over a period of huge success. It was an exciting time to be at the club. 'United were going well when I joined, and it was all a bit of a fairy tale that within a few months we had won the Premiership, the FA Cup and the European Champions League in amazing style,' he said. 'You never forget experiences like that, and I am grateful to have been a part of it all.'

McClaren was not just along for the ride. He took on the first-team coaching from his first day at the club and made a major contribution. McClaren had studied, and still does study, the coaching methods of top foreign bosses, drawing from them any techniques that he can adapt to English football. And Manchester United certainly benefited from his coaching abilities, the team retaining the championship in the 1999–2000 and 2000–01 seasons.

It was not only at club level that he was making his mark, though. The Football Association also recognised his talents, and he was invited to join the coaching team for the national squad. When Kevin Keegan resigned as England manager, McClaren found himself sharing the caretaker manager role with Peter Taylor until the arrival of Sven-Göran Eriksson.

McClaren's involvement with England was probably the start of the parting of the ways with United. There was no direct conflict of interests, but attending national-team coaching sessions did detract a little from his Old Trafford duties. The club were supportive at first but became impatient, and it became clear that it was going to turn into an either/or situation.

McClaren had grown more ambitious as his coaching confidence grew, and the suggestion that he would one day step into Fergie's shoes as manager of Manchester United must have appealed a great deal. But it gradually became clear that the suggestion was unlikely to become a reality. Although Ferguson was due to retire in 2002 at that point, it seemed more likely that the board would appoint a big-name coach to replace him. McClaren was growing in stature but had no direct management experience, and it is unlikely that the Manchester faithful would have accepted him as Fergie's replacement.

It became obvious that McClaren would have to move away from Old Trafford to break into management. And when word reached Fergie that several clubs were interested in signing McClaren as their manager, he did not stand in his way. It was an interesting reaction from the United boss, because he clearly valued his number two and could have easily issued a 'hands off' message to other clubs. But Ferguson recognised the need for McClaren to fulfil his management potential. Far from shouting his indignation at losing his right-hand man, Ferguson encouraged him and wished him well.

Middlesbrough beat various others, including Southampton and West Ham, to the signing of McClaren as their boss, and in June 2001, he walked into the Riverside Stadium as the new manager. Back at Old Trafford, Ferguson declined to find a new assistant and elevated coach Jim Ryan to the job as a temporary measure until his own future was decided. Ferguson's retirement was just one season away, and any new manager would want to bring in his own men, so there was little point in finding a new number two from outside the club at that stage.

Installed in his new position in the North-east, McClaren found himself with the full managerial load to carry, instead of just being able to concentrate on coaching. He had to trim the Middlesbrough wage bill, talk to the media and generally do all the things which keep managers away from the training pitch. This side of the job came as something of a surprise to him: 'Working closely with managers prepares you for the extra work in a sense, but when you are the one who actually has the ultimate responsibility and the decisions, it is different, and nothing totally prepares you for that.'

Middlesbrough struggled at first under their new boss, but gradually the new coaching style made a difference, and the side gained confidence. Results also improved, and the side established mid-table safety. And with McClaren gone, it was clear that United were struggling to find the same form that had been achieved while he was coaching them. Could it be that he was being missed?

Boro even went on to reach the semi-final of the FA Cup and were only narrowly beaten by Arsenal when Gianluca Festa put the ball in his own net. The big news coming out of Old Trafford was that Sir Alex Ferguson had changed his mind about retiring and would be staying on for the foreseeable future. United rallied as a result, and the season ended with Fergie and McClaren both happy men.

Things were going well for McClaren at Middlesbrough, and so any suggestion that he might be heading for the Elland Road hot seat when David O'Leary left Leeds United in July 2002 was soon extinguished. But not before some serious soul-searching and a phone call to his old boss. It seems that Fergie advised his ex-assistant to take the Leeds job if it was offered, even though he knew that the Yorkshire giants would prove to be stiffer opposition if McClaren was in charge. There were suggestions that a deal was done but newspaper reports revealed too much too soon and McClaren decided to end speculation by declaring his immediate future with Middlesbrough.

The progress at the Riverside continued, and the League Cup was won during the 2003–04 season, the first trophy in the club's history. It was party time again for Steve McClaren. As a result of this win, Middlesbrough also qualified for the UEFA Cup in 2004–05 and competed in Europe for the first time. McClaren's experience in Europe with Manchester United proved invaluable, and his side made it to the quarter-finals, beating Lazio 2–0 at the Riverside along the way. The team also secured their best ever Premiership finish, finishing seventh and qualifying for the UEFA Cup once again.

The team's second attempt at European success produced some breathtaking moments for the fans. In the second leg of the quarter-final tie against Basel at the Riverside, McClaren's team found themselves needing to score four times with just over an hour left to play. They looked dead and buried, but a Mark Viduka strike before half-time gave the side hope. The boss had been part of a remarkable European turnaround before when United won the Champions League in 1999, and he must have infused his players with a belief that they could complete the comeback. A further goal from Viduka followed by one from Jimmy Floyd Hasselbaink set the stage for Massimo Maccarone to score a dramatic 90th-minute winner. Middlesbrough were through to the semis.

When Boro found themselves in exactly the same position in the second leg of the semi-final at the Riverside against Steaua Bucharest – needing four goals to win with just over an hour to play – nobody thought that lightning would strike twice. However, McClaren's team once again found it within themselves to pull off an unlikely comeback, scoring four goals and securing a place in the UEFA Cup final against Seville.

Although the players must take great credit for their strength of character and perseverance against all odds, McClaren's role cannot be overlooked. The manager was the picture of calm on the touchline for both games, and instead of accepting defeat – as many would have done faced with the same situation – he made important substitutions and tactical changes that turned the game in his side's favour. He had seen what could be achieved with some proactive substitutions when he worked for Fergie, and realised that he had to act. It demonstrated a determination and conviction that Fergie would have been proud of.

It is also possible, of course, that he had learned what not to do from Sven-Göran Eriksson, who has been castigated in the past for his inability to make personnel and tactical changes during the course of a match. McClaren was sitting alongside Eriksson when England were eliminated by ten-man Brazil during the 2002 World Cup. Trailing by two goals to one with half an hour to play, England were given a lifeline when Brazilian playmaker Ronaldinho was harshly sent off. However, rather than take advantage of the numerical advantage that had been gifted to his team, Eriksson failed to change the shape of his side and waited until there were just over ten minutes to play before using his final two substitutions. Whether any intervention would have made a difference is impossible to say, but McClaren would have been well aware of the consequences of both action and inaction in difficult situations because of his previous experiences.

This point was further highlighted when England lost to Northern Ireland in a 2005 World Cup Qualifier match. It was Steve McClaren who was tearing his hair out and yelling at the players while Sven calmly sat in the dugout looking like a lost undertaker. TV pundit Ian Wright commented, 'You would think that it was Steve who was the manager. He was the bloke trying to change things to get a result. He was doing all the things you expect from a manager, while Sven was just sitting there like an FA official.'

It was a comment and view shared by many, and Steve McClaren's name was increasingly touted as a future England manager. When it was announced that Sven was stepping down from the position, it seemed that McClaren's appointment as the next England boss would be sooner rather than later. And while it must have been a blow to Middlesbrough when he left, it would certainly have renewed faith among the supporters of the national side.

It will, of course, take all his skills and experience to ensure success in his new role. The England manager is subject to a huge amount of scrutiny from the press and there are few opportunities for success – unlike a club side, the national team only get the chance to win silverware once every two years. McClaren seems as though he is the sort of person who will deal well with the pressure, though. There is even a suggestion that McClaren thrives on such situations. Any hints that he picked up from Fergie for dealing with high-pressure scenarios will need to be put into good effect in the coming years.

However, there are those who believe that McClaren took more to the Theatre of Dreams than he brought away, although that is not his own view. 'I learned a great deal from Alex,' he admitted in a TV interview when he was still manager at the Riverside. 'He is a winner, and he has proved himself at more than one club, although United has been the biggest, of course. He never lacks determination, and he expects the same from his players. When you see what he has won over the years, you cannot query how he does things, just that he has found a formula that definitely works for him.

'Although you can learn so much from him, you cannot copy what another man does, because we are all different in character, but you can see what works and adapt it to your own approach.

'His pre-match talks were worth hearing. Alex always reminded players that winning is about taking opportunities when they arise. He said that before every game, and I do the same at Middlesbrough. Sometimes you only get one chance in an entire match, and you have to take it. You don't have time to think about it. Alex tells his players to anticipate and to be ready to pounce at any time during the 90 minutes, and that is sound advice. It is what wins matches, and we all want that, so it is good to pass that on to your players.

'You have to have tactics, plans and schemes, but the most successful coaches are those who get inside their players' heads, and Alex certainly does that. He is a master of psychology, both with his own players and also with the opposition. He knows exactly how to give a player confidence and how to place doubt in the minds of the opposition.'

McClaren is another ex-associate of Ferguson who has taken advantage of his former boss's willingness to help: 'Alex is always at the end of the phone, too. He doesn't mind you phoning him for advice. I always found that he was amenable to passing on tips, and I certainly felt the benefit of having worked with him.'

As a student of the game, he has learned much from Sir Alex. Anyone doubting that need only look at his success with Middlesbrough, both at home and in Europe. And McClaren is always open to learning new things, just as Fergie has been throughout his career. It is for this reason that McClaren undertook a UEFA Pro Licence course in July 2005 at Warwick University. He is still hungry to learn and to hear new thoughts, and he believes you go on learning. 'I don't think you should ever want to stop trying to improve and to learn new ideas,' he said. 'If you come away with just one thing which you can make work at your club, then it has all been worthwhile. I am up for any course, because I don't believe anyone knows all there is to know. Something learned is something gained and will perhaps provide just that slight difference between winning and not winning.

'The person who stops trying to learn is the person who is standing still, and whatever sport you are in, you cannot just stand still. Everyone else will overtake you. The top foreign coaches never believe they know it all, and they are constantly seeking new ways to gain an edge and get the best from their players. That is why they are so successful in European competitions. We have some good young managers coming through, and we can rival those foreign coaches – but not if we are not willing to learn.'

This openness to continually learning more about the game will stand McClaren in good stead and is perhaps one of the reasons Fergie once said, 'He has impressed me a lot, both during matches and on the training ground. I believe he will go on to achieve great things.' Just how great remains to be seen, but if he wins England their first major trophy since 1966, the Auld Enemy will owe a debt of gratitude to Sir Alex Ferguson.

10

BEHIND THE SCENES

SOME OF THE LESS HIGH-PROFILE PLAYERS WHO HAVE PLAYED UNDER FERGIE HAVE also continued to be a part of the game and are still carrying forward the lessons they learned from their old boss. Interestingly, some of them are still plying their trade at Old Trafford, so in addition to passing on what they have already learned from the Govan maestro, they are still observing how he operates.

In the past, clubs have often promoted from within, Liverpool and United being good examples. In Liverpool's case, the 'boot room' was a source of success, providing a succession of managers from Shankly onwards and contributing to the most triumphant period in the club's history. United's attempts at creating a similar dynasty in the past have not been so successful, but Fergie has put together a new team of unsung heroes behind the scenes at Old Trafford.

Brian McClair is one of those unsung heroes, a player blessed not only with great skill but also with intelligence over and above your footballing average. These days he is director of the Youth

Academy at Old Trafford and has fulfilled various coaching roles. Unlikely though it might seem, McClair could be a dark horse in the stakes to replace Fergie. He might not want the job at the moment but such a challenge would be hard to resist for someone who is such an important part of the club.

McClair was one of Fergie's best buys and quite a bargain; he joined from Celtic in July 1987 for £850,000, which was a pretty reasonable price for a proven goal scorer. He was Ferguson's second signing for United, Viv Anderson having been the first. Anderson was a great servant, but if comparisons need be made, McClair was even better because he proved to be more than just a scoring talent. He was also a great playmaker who could read a game well and quickly see the opposition's vulnerable spots.

'I knew a lot about Brian from Scotland,' said Fergie in a tribute to the player when he hung up his boots. 'He had made a big impression on me when I was at Aberdeen. He was a fluid player who always moved when his team had the ball. I was impressed with his running ability and, of course, with his goals.

'When I joined United, I knew his contract with Celtic was close to renewal, so I had him in mind as a signing. We worked hard to get him, but he was well worth it. I came to trust him with many duties. He never let me down and has proved to be a great servant to Manchester United both on and off the pitch.'

Brian McClair was born in Airdrie on 8 December 1963 and surprisingly began his career as an apprentice at Aston Villa. He was not there for long, though. The call of Scotland was too strong, and Brian joined Motherwell as a youngster in August 1981. It was there that he really started to learn his trade as a footballer while studying maths at Glasgow University. He gained a degree, too.

McClair was an academic who could have succeeded in any number of careers had he not made it as a professional footballer.

There were even some newspaper suggestions at the time of his retirement from playing that he could have become a politician. But, as it happened, he did make it in football, and during his playing days with club and country, he earned himself a great reputation as an intelligent player. His progress was quick, and in June 1983, Celtic paid £75,000 for him, a lot of cash for a 19 year old.

After scoring 98 goals in 129 league games for the Hoops and having been named Scottish Football Writers' Association Player of the Year and Scottish Players' Player of the Year in 1987, McClair signed for United. He won most of the domestic honours the game could offer with the Reds and finally decided to move back to Motherwell as a player–coach at the end of the 1997–98 season. His final appearance for United was as a substitute in a 3–0 home win over Leeds United. Ironically, his first playing season had seen United finish as runners-up in the league, and his last season saw them finish as runners-up again, this time in the Premiership.

'I have no complaints,' he said at the time of his retirement. 'Football was good to me, and in playing for Celtic and Manchester United as well as for Scotland, I had the honour of being with the two biggest clubs in Britain as well as playing for my country. It doesn't get much better than that.'

As for his international career of thirty caps and two goals, former Scotland manager Andy Roxburgh said he was one of the most reliable players he ever encountered. 'It was not that he was a spectacular player,' said Andy. 'He did score some spectacular goals, but he was never the kind of player who would come off the bench in the late stages of the game and turn it all round for you. He made his impression throughout the 90 minutes. He was thoughtful, never stopped working and could control a game. He was one of those players you wish could go on for ever.'

After a short spell as player–coach with Motherwell, McClair then joined Blackburn Rovers as a coach in 1998, appointed by Brian Kidd when he took over as manager at Ewood Park following the departure of Roy Hodgson. The Blackburn Rovers story was not a successful one, and Brian McClair returned to Old Trafford as reserve-team coach in 2001 before taking over responsibility for the youth team.

'I enjoy coaching and you could not get any better facilities than at Old Trafford,' McClair said when he accepted a coaching job with United. 'It is good to help young players start their careers and be able to help them not only with their various skills but also to be able to get the best out of their careers. It is the philosophy of the boss that young players must be given every possible chance. He believes it is only fair to them and that we would be doing less than the best for the club if we did not see their fullest potential realised.'

The need to nurture young talent may seem obvious, but Fergie has always prioritised this requirement as vital for his teams, and for the whole game, when other managers have been content to buy in their talent. He has always emphasised the detailed care of his young players, and many of Fergie's disciples have taken this element of his approach on themselves. For example, the appointment of Steve McClaren was partly due to his experience of bringing through young players. Brian Barwick said, 'Steve believes in the nurturing of young talent – and especially young English talent – and giving those players an early chance.'

McClair has also become expert in youth development, Kieran Richardson being the most obvious youth-team graduate to have benefited from being coached by the intelligent Scot. But it is not just in coaching that McClair is proving himself. As reserve-team manager in 2004–05, his side won an unprecedented four trophies: the Pontins' Holidays League, the FA Premier Reserve

League, The Pontins' Holidays League Cup and the Premier Reserve League Playoff. Although he has never tried his hand as the manager of a senior side, there is time for him to yet take the plunge. If he does, it seems likely that he will put into practice some of the things he has learned, having identified what it is that makes Sir Alex so special. 'His care of his players is very important to him,' said McClair. 'He might give you a roasting himself, but woe betide anyone else who might try it. He is very loyal to those who are loyal to him, and he wants only the very best for his players.

'His knowledge of the game is immense, and he is tactically very shrewd. He leaves very little to chance and works hard to make sure that his players and the rest of the staff are fully prepared for each and every game, no matter who you are playing and in what competition. Winning matters to him, and he does everything possible to make it happen. I think that he gives a great example to all those around him. If you want to be successful, you have to work for it.'

Perhaps we shall see Brian McClair become number two at Old Trafford one of these days, and then who knows what might happen? He certainly has the credentials, a good brain, the ears of the players and the supporters, and, of course, a portion of the Fergie legacy to bring to the table, to go on to greater things. And if he ever became caretaker manager, it would take a strong contender to shift him from the job.

Mike Phelan is another important name behind the scenes at Old Trafford. Like McClair, Phelan is a former United player and a good servant to the club. At the coaching ground he has been a rising star and has also been speculatively linked with the eventual manager's vacancy by some of the more unrealistic press men, although he might prefer to go on coaching since it has been so much a part of his life already.

Mike Phelan is a Lancashire lad through and through, having been born in Nelson in September 1962. He joined Burnley as an apprentice in 1979 and became a full-time professional a year later. Thus began a career that would eventually lead to him becoming part of the furniture at Old Trafford.

In 1985, Phelan left Burnley to join Norwich and was part of the same squad as Steve Bruce. Phelan impressed throughout his stay at Carrow Road, and Ferguson landed another bargain when he paid £750,000 for him in July 1989. 'Knowing I was joining Manchester United was just incredible,' said Phelan. 'Norwich had been marvellous for me and is still one of the nicest clubs in the game, but Manchester United is the club of dreams. When you arrive at Old Trafford, you know you have joined the most famous football club in the world.'

He made his United debut on August 1989 in the opening game of the season, which ended in a sensational 4–1 victory over Arsenal. Considering that the Gunners were reigning champions, it was electrifying stuff. 'I remember the game well,' said Phelan in an interview with the *Manchester Evening News* when he returned to Old Trafford as coach. 'The boss got the tactics exactly right, and Arsenal did not know what had hit them. It was a brilliant game in which to make your United debut.'

Mike Phelan remained as a United player until 1994, and during that time, he won every domestic medal, the European Cup-Winners' Cup and was even capped by England against Italy. 'He was a great utility player,' said Fergie. 'We first signed him because he could play in midfield or in defence with equal ability, and that is important. I think the bonus with Mike was the fact that he had such energy and would keep going right to the end. He was never lazy and always willing to give an honest, hard-working performance. You need players like that in a side.'

Phelan left Old Trafford to return to Norwich as coach under

Gary Megson. When Megson moved on to Blackpool and then Stockport, Phelan went with him. He then returned to Old Trafford in 2000 and took charge of teams at various levels until being appointed first-team coach after the departure of Steve McClaren.

His coaching role brings him into very close contact with Fergie, who likes things to be done his way. Therefore, the Fergie way has become the Phelan way. Not that Mike is not his own man, but he is smart enough to know what works. He also appreciates the position he is in. 'I always wanted to be a coach, and I feel fortunate to have been able to gain experience at various clubs and now to have become established with Manchester United,' he said. 'It is a fantastic experience to be here and working with the first team. It is great to be involved with the biggest of clubs, and I don't think there is a day goes by when you don't learn something new.

'There is a much greater emphasis these days on technique, but fitness is also vitally important. Much greater care is now taken over training, diet, rest and overall preparation. The boss is very big on preparation, both for the team as a whole and for each individual player.

'I don't think that it is fully recognised that Sir Alex is not just about today and the next result, he is about tomorrow, too. It is no coincidence that United have a great run for a number of years then a brief lull in success and then win everything again.

'He is a man with a mission to not only win today but to create what will win tomorrow. The club has a constant hunger for success, and Sir Alex is just the man to not only fuel that hunger but make sure it is fulfilled as well.'

Mike Phelan is now respected as one of the best coaches in the British game. Whether he wishes to move in to management one day remains to be seen, but there is less opportunity for hands-on coaching when you are the boss, so he might prefer to stay where he is. He would also probably have to move on from Old Trafford to have a chance of being a manager in his own right, but if he did, there is little doubt that the things he has learned working alongside Fergie would be used to good effect.

Carlos Queiroz is the man Sir Alex Ferguson has allegedly recommended as his replacement when the time comes, and it is true that he is certainly a beneficiary of the legacy having worked side by side with Britain's most successful soccer boss in recent years. Born in Nampala, Mozambique, in March 1953, Queiroz made his mark as a player but even more so as a coach. His first major success was in coaching Portugal's Under-21 side to the World Youth Championship in 1989. His reputation was greatly enhanced after that triumph, especially as he made a major contribution to the careers of stars like Luís Figo, Rui Costa, Jorge Costa and João Pinto.

Queiroz has travelled extensively, perhaps indicating that he is a restless soul still trying to find his dream job. In 1993, he was appointed manager of the Portugal national side. He did well but gave up after a year to become boss of Sporting Lisbon. He was manager of Sporting for nearly two years before leaving to coach the New York/New Jersey Metrostars in the United States. After a year, he was at the airport again, this time flying to Japan where he was appointed boss of Nagoya Grampus Eight. He spent a year in Japan before resuming his round the world in 80 jobs tour in the Middle East, where he became manager of the United Arab Emirates national team. In 1999, he packed his bags again and headed for South Africa to become manager of their national side. He stayed for nearly two years and saw the team qualify for the 2002 World Cup before resigning just before the competition.

Queiroz arrived at Old Trafford in the summer of 2002 and was appointed as assistant manager. It all seemed to be going very well when he received an offer from Real Madrid to become their new manager and packed his bags again. But his time in charge of Real Madrid was not a success, and after just ten months, he left the club and returned to Old Trafford to team up once again with Sir Alex. 'I like it at Manchester United, because everything is so professional, and there is so much talent here,' he said on his return to the club. 'My role is to supply the technique of modern football. The game has changed and continues to change, and you have to keep up to date with all that is happening as well as put into practice ideas of your own which will keep your team ahead of the others. Working with Sir Alex is a wonderful experience, because he thinks football but in a very productive way. He does not like to lose, even though he has already won everything. That approach cannot be bettered, and he makes sure that the fire he has is in his players too.'

Ferguson obviously rates his number two highly, otherwise he would not have welcomed him back after his spell with Real Madrid. 'He has a lot of international experience, and in today's football, you need that,' said Fergie. 'Manchester United has to think global, and someone like Carlos Queiroz, who has experienced football at various levels in various parts of the world, is a very useful asset.'

But could Queiroz hack it as manager? Could he really be the man who will take Manchester United on to more success? If nothing else, he has two important factors in his favour. One is that he has worked closely with Fergie for a number of years now and would provide continuity, and the other is that he is used to criticism. As he said himself, 'Criticism is for me inspirational. It is a driving force, so I do not turn away from it, I use it to thrive.' Having a thick skin is surely one of the most important assets for any man who would be king at the Theatre of Dreams.

McClair, Phelan and Queiroz, working behind the scenes to

ensure the continued success of Manchester United, are all beneficiaries of Fergie's legacy. Perhaps one of them will eventually become the main man at Old Trafford, but whether or not they do, there is no doubt that working on the coaching, man management and match preparation with their boss on a daily basis must surely have given them an edge for their future careers. They not only know what it is like to win but also what it is like to be in charge of the team everyone else wants to beat. They all have the same determination, pride and overwhelming will to win. To be chosen to take on such responsibility demonstrates the high esteem in which Fergie holds them. He only chooses to work with those who share his passion and ideals, and would not place his faith in men who weren't up to the job. It is perhaps for this reason above all others that the current back-room staff are so well placed to spread the Fergie gospel for many years to come.

But they are not the only ones who are likely to benefit from having worked alongside the fiery Scot. There are a number of players who have played for Ferguson – or are still playing for him – who will doubtless go on to become managers themselves and will surely use their share of Fergie's legacy to good effect.

Roy Keane may have left the club under a cloud of controversy, but he is an obvious choice to fall into the category of ex-players most likely to succeed in management. He has played for two of the finest and most successful bosses in the game and has never flinched from saying his piece about managers, fellow players or opponents. But far from being simply an aggressive footballer who seeks victory at any cost, Keane has a good brain and exceptional football pedigree.

Born in August 1971, Keane did not set the academic world on fire while he was at school. His passion was passing a ball rather than passing exams, but he was far from thick. He had the capability to do well but wasn't interested in his studies and was determined to have a career in football instead, as he revealed to me in an early interview at Nottingham Forest.

He chose wisely, although it did not appear so at first. Keane wrote to all the major clubs asking for a trial but had no luck. 'Not getting a good reponse from the clubs I wrote to was very disappointing,' he said. 'Among others, I had a nice letter from Nottingham Forest, who let me down gently. I joined Cobh Ramblers and took a soccer course to improve my play and fitness, and then the unexpected happened when a scout from Forest saw me play and invited me to Nottingham for a trial.'

He spent a week in Nottingham but did not have the opportunity to play a match, his time being mostly spent with Archie Gemmill, the youth coach, who simply put him through his paces in the daily training sessions. Keane travelled home feeling that it had all been a waste of time, but after a short time, he was contacted again and asked to return for another session, this time to include a match for the reserves.

As a result, Keane joined Forest and was plunged into the first team at Anfield for his debut with only one hour's notice. Thus started an incredible few years at the City ground with Brian Clough as his boss. 'Brian Clough was an amazing manager,' said Keane. 'He totally did his own thing and did not do it by the book at all. He was great for me, because he was not only a very good team manager but he understood individual characters and their needs. He was a winner too and performed miracles with both Forest and Derby. You learn a lot from people like that.'

Elevation to the Republic of Ireland national side was a natural side effect of his progress under Clough. Jack Charlton handed Keane his international debut, but it has been well recorded that the combative midfielder was less than impressed by Charlton, or by his successor Mick McCarthy. Big Jack became a national hero in Ireland, because of his success with the team, but Keane has never attempted to hide his lack of respect for Charlton and his methods of play and man management. Keane was also famously thrown out of the Republic of Ireland's 2002 World Cup squad after criticising McCarthy and the team's preparations.

Keane joined United in 1993 for a transfer fee of £3.75 million. It seems like a bargain now but was big money then and made him the most expensive player in the British game. Since then, Keane has won just about every medal going. Although suspension meant that he was unable to play in the famous European Cup final in 1999, he had played in every game leading up to the dramatic final. Despite his massive contribution to the campaign as a whole, he had to be persuaded to go and get his medal. He had earned it, but his pride made him reluctant to accept any reward that he did not feel was wholly justified, a pride not dissimilar to Fergie's.

As captain, Keane found himself working more and more closely with Sir Alex, discussing the opposition, tactics, team options and the approach to each game. Although it seemed inevitable that he would move on towards the end of his career, his transfer to Celtic was rather sudden. Even though the door seemed to slam behind him, you cannot help but think that he has been given the key to return one day if he decides that coaching and management will be his next step. Certainly, any rifts were healed by the testimonial for Keane held at Old Trafford at the end of the 2005–06 season.

'Roy's qualities of leadership are plain for all to see,' said Fergie when discussing the loss of Keane before the 1999 Champions League final. 'That has been his greatest role in recent times, and I believe he has the qualifications, the determination and the experience of football at the highest level to become a very good manager in the future.'

Neither of them is likely to engage in a mutual admiration society, but Keane has been equally praising of his old boss to whom he has remained loyal, the kind of loyalty that Fergie himself has demonstrated many times to those whom he really respects. 'My respect for the boss is absolute,' Keane said. 'He has proved time and time again that he is one of the very best in the game. He knows about man management, he has a head full of tactics to suit all occasions and he has created several championship teams. Doing it once is quite an achievement, but doing it several times is fantastic. His psychology is second to none, and he has a tremendous will to win, even now after he has won everything. I can relate to a lot of his character.'

Whatever Roy Keane chooses to do once he hangs up his boots, he will take with him the knowledge he has accrued from the various managers he has played for in his career but in particular that gained while working with Ferguson.

But Keane is not the only one of the game's senior players who may one day venture into management. Ryan Giggs might not seem a likely candidate at first glance but, then, neither did Mark Hughes. They both seemed to express themselves on the pitch but remain quiet and almost withdrawn off it. The working relationship between Giggs and Ferguson has been a close one ever since the Welsh star was signed by United. Much has rubbed off, and when Ryan can no longer fly down the wing giving opposition defenders blurred vision, he might well find himself pursuing a career in management.

Born in Cardiff in November 1973, Ryan Giggs has more playing years behind him than ahead of him, but what fantastic years they have been. As a teenager playing in the first team ahead of schedule, he was protected from the media by his boss and from losing his level-headedness by his mother. 'I would go home from training, and on the way, I would see the newspaper headlines about me and maybe a big advertising hoarding with my picture on it,' he said. 'When I got home, my mother would tell me to do the washing-up. It was her way of making sure that I did not get carried away and start to believe my own publicity.'

While Giggs's mum kept his head right, Ferguson kept his protégé's career on the right track, and he has won everything there is to win in club football – UEFA Cup and European Cup-Winners' Cup medals being the exception, but who needs those when you have a Champions League medal? He has performed well on the international stage with Wales, although it does seem an injustice that he has never taken part in the finals of the World Cup or European Championships. Some critics have even commented that it is a pity he is Welsh, but Ryan is always quick to reject that claim. He has been very happy to play for Wales, even though he could have played for England and would have taken part in the tournaments which have eluded him.

Ferguson has a soft spot for Giggs, having seen his whole career unfold. 'Ryan is the longest-serving player at Old Trafford,' said Fergie. 'I have known him boy and man and seen his career develop to a brilliant level. He always looked like a professional footballer, as if he was created especially for the job.

'It is not just his obvious skill but the constant strain he puts on defences until they crack – perhaps for a teammate, but they crack anyway. He still has tremendous skill and a good brain.'

Giggs has obviously benefited from working alongside Ferguson, and if he does go into management, he will take with him an insight into one of the greatest talents a manager can possess. 'I think the boss is the best of them all at motivation,' he said. 'He knows how to motivate a team, and he knows how to motivate individuals. He gives what is needed at exactly the right time. He doesn't always rant, sometimes a quiet but telling word does the trick. Look at his record as a manager. It speaks for itself.'

Ryan Giggs is well placed to benefit from Fergie's legacy, because he has worked for him for his whole career. It is Ferguson's methods and approach to the game that Giggs has had the most exposure to, and it is these that he would surely emulate if he goes down the coaching route himself. Although the two men have contrasting personalities, Giggs is perhaps the best exponent of Fergie's football philosophy and as such would be an ideal candidate to carry on his work in the future.

Ole Gunnar Solskjær is yet another who is tipped to go into management by no less than Sir Alex himself. 'He has great coaching potential,' said Fergie. 'I do believe that Ole has the qualities that will make him successful off the pitch when he has finished playing. I can see him as a coach, and he has the playing experience and the respect of players which will make a big difference to his future career.'

Solskjær was born in Kristiansund, Norway, in February 1973 and made a name for himself with Norwegian third-division side Clausenegen FK before moving to Molde, one of the country's leading clubs. His reputation as a top scorer soon had clubs from all over Europe watching him, but it was Fergie who nipped in with £1.5 million to sign him. That was in the summer of 1996, and it really was one of Fergie's best buys: Solskjær scored on his debut and went on to bag many more vital goals, including the famous Champions League winner.

'Joining Manchester United was the best thing that ever happened to me,' Solskjær said. 'Not only did I become part of the biggest club in the world, but I have had the honour of playing alongside many great players and working for a great manager.

'Sir Alex knows football inside out, and he knows his players as individuals. I have learned much from him about tactics and motivation and preparing for a big match. Perhaps I will become a coach one day. I enjoy that side of the game and I have learned much to help me.'

The latter years have seen him struggling to get back into action after long-term injuries but that time may have proved beyond any doubt that his future lies in coaching and management. His quick-witted approach to football suggests that he will have keenly observed the coaching skills, man management and timely tactical substitutions of which Fergie is a master. Ole has proved himself to be a super sub, but there may be no substitution for him when he ventures into serious coaching and management.

Gary Neville has earned himself an excellent reputation as a player for Manchester United and England. There can be no contesting the fact that he has quietly and without fuss been one of the best full-backs in world football for the last decade and more. Could that talent be turned into the kind of qualities needed to be a successful manager?

Neville was born in Bury in February 1975, his brother Phil coming along a couple of years later. They were both products of the successful United youth team. Gary made his first-team debut as a substitute in September 1992 only a few months after he had captained the youth team to the FA Youth Cup. He was not a first-team regular for a while but continued to progress and eventually established himself as one of the first names on the team sheet. He has captained the side, and there is no question that the United defence is a safer place with him in it. The attack has more bite too, since his forays along the right wing have resulted in many scoring opportunities. He has pace, he can beat players and can cross accurately. You cannot ask for more from a modern-day full-back.

There is much more to Gary Neville than that, though. His father has been in football administration for years, and he knows how the game works off the pitch. He has often been a players' spokesman, both at Old Trafford and with the England set-up, something to which Ferguson can relate because he often adopted that role himself when he was a player. In fact, Ferguson has great respect for Neville, who is another that he believes could become a successful manager. 'Gary has the ability and the knowledge and determination,' he said. 'He is a thinking player, and I am sure he will go on to become a very good coach and manager.'

Neville is still chiefly concerned with continuing to play as long as possible. 'I am a Manchester United player and will go on being so as long as they want me,' he said. 'I know that one day I shall have to do something else, but I would like to stay in football, and if that means coaching or management, then I would probably give it a go. It is hard to think of life away from Old Trafford, but who knows?'

Perhaps Neville will not have to contemplate life away from Old Trafford. The natural move would be for him to begin a coaching career at the club and progress from there. Many of Fergie's ex-captains have become managers themselves, and it seems that Neville is well placed to continue that tradition.

It is incredible to think that Teddy Sheringham was born before England won the World Cup in 1966, yet he is still playing in the Premiership and scoring valuable goals. When he joined Manchester United from Spurs in 1997 for £3.5 million, he was already 31 and had a tough act to follow, being brought in to replace the prematurely retired Eric Cantona. Needless to say, Sheringham's first season was not a huge success, but by the time he had moved on again a few years later, he had become something of a hero, not least because of his great contribution to United winning the Champions League.

It is probably easier to list the clubs for whom Sheringham has not played than those he has, but everywhere he has gone he has proved to be a player who can score goals. He also has great vision and is a tremendous playmaker. That shows a good brain and therefore suggests he could be management material.

'Sheringham had both the skills and the perception to win

games,' said Ferguson. 'He was not another Eric Cantona; he was his own man but could turn a game with one well-timed and unexpected pass.'

Teddy Sheringham is a thinking player's player, and that is what makes him a likely candidate for success in the management hot seat. He also learned from Sir Alex how to carefully select his players and motivate them. 'I think I saw in him a man who knew how to get the best from his players,' said Sheringham. 'Yes, he would give you a full blasting when you didn't deliver, but he did his best to help you perform well, so there was no excuse if you didn't play your part. His match preparation was excellent, and his psychology was brilliant. You cannot fail to learn from a manager like that.

'He was not at all like Brian Clough, who was my boss at Forest. Clough was really relaxed and laid back, while Fergie rarely seemed to relax. Yet both men were winners. If I ever go into coaching or management, I shall have learned quite a lot from them both.'

Denis Irwin served Manchester United from 1990 before heading for pastures new at Wolves in 2002. The impact he made at Old Trafford was tremendous, and he is still sorely missed. Like Roy Keane, Denis was born in Cork and was always destined for great things in football, although it did not seem that his career was going to flourish when he was released by Leeds in 1986 at the age of 23. Oldham had no hesitation in signing him, and Denis came of age there before signing for United in June 1990 for £650,000. What followed was a decade of success with both his club and the Republic of Ireland. When Roy Keane signed for United, Denis was an obvious room-mate choice, and he played a great part in helping the fellow Cork man to settle at the club.

Nobody who has seen Denis play would question his ability. He provided great service on the left, both as a tough-tackling defender and as an attacker. He could also take a great free-kick, even before Beckham started to bend it. His natural ability was not lost on Ferguson. 'I would say that Denis Irwin is one of the best left-flank players I have ever seen, and I mean in terms of world football,' said Sir Alex. 'He was not only very talented but a thinking player, and you don't often find such a combination of abilities.'

Whether or not Irwin finds himself in charge of a team one day, he has certainly appreciated playing for Fergie. 'He is a great manager – the best,' said Denis. 'I don't know what the future holds for me, but the experience of playing for Sir Alex is not one you forget. He was meticulous about everything and everyone. No stone was left unturned in the will to win, and I think that is a great lesson for anyone wanting to think about management. If you anticipate well and cover all possibilities, you have to be successful eventually.'

Denis Irwin could be a dark horse in the management stakes and one day emerge as a very successful boss indeed. He certainly learned well and cherishes his share of the Fergie legacy.

You cannot discuss Fergie and Manchester United without giving mention to David Beckham. Somehow it does not seem likely that Beckham will ever join the ranks of managers, but, then, the same was said many years ago about Kevin Keegan. It will either be a clean break, or he will try his hand as a boss. If he chooses the latter course, he has not only his own talent and a wealth of experience at various levels but also the knowledge of working with Sir Alex Ferguson to boot.

The apparent falling out between Fergie and Beckham was unfortunate to say the least, especially as Ferguson had fulfilled a father-like role in Beckham's development from youth player to world icon. Beckham was not given preferential treatment, but there is no doubt he benefited from individual coaching, something in which Fergie firmly believes.

Beckham has learned the importance of bringing on young players from his old boss, and has already opened football academies in London and Los Angeles. He has also learned about motivation. Watch him lead by example on the pitch and you can see the Ferguson influence at work.

The example of Fergie's success might just draw Beckham into the challenge of football management when his playing days are over. It may seem unlikely at present, but people change, and when it appears that players have turned their back on football, they have a habit of rushing back to its supposed security. Despite all the media attention that surrounds Beckham and his personal life, his first love is football. And if he does return to Old Trafford as manager one day, perhaps people will talk of Sir Matt Busby, Sir Bobby Charlton, Sir Alex Ferguson *and* Sir David Beckham.

11

ONE LAST TIME?

FERGIE MUST HAVE SEEN HIS WHOLE CAREER PASS BEFORE HIS EYES SEVERAL TIMES during the 2005–06 season. It was another roller-coaster campaign with the usual ups and downs that have come to characterise his stewardship of the Manchester giants. Along the way, there was the anguish of an early exit from Europe; the heart-in-mouth Premiership and cup campaigns; calls for his retirement; the sour ending to the reign of Roy Keane as captain; the bedding in of new players; and, to cap it all, the suggestion that he might become the new England manager.

However, at one point it wasn't even certain that Fergie would be around for the 2005–06 season. In May 2005, after having watched his side lose to Arsenal in the FA Cup final – resulting in a trophyless campaign – and having seen the club return to private ownership under Malcolm Glazer, it seemed entirely possible that Ferguson would retire from football. In particular, the shock and disappointment of losing the cup final on penalties despite outplaying the Gunners throughout the game could have proved to be too much for a lesser man to cope with. Many managers would have been tempted to call it a day, content with the knowledge that even those who are devoutly opposed to Manchester United had to admit that Arsenal's victory was a total travesty. But that was not good enough for Fergie. With the bit between his teeth, he set about planning for another year at the helm. There was silverware to be won, points to be proven and justice to be had.

With the takeover by the Glazer family completed towards the end of the 2004–05 season, there were fears that they would clamp down on any spending by the manager in the close season. Joel Glazer, one of Malcolm Glazer's sons and a non-executive director on the Manchester United board, was quick to dispel any fears. 'We are going to provide the manager with the resources necessary to field the best team,' he said. 'It is very frustrating when I read about hands being tied. It doesn't matter what the situation is, there has to be some restraint, but if the manager feels a situation is right, then the board has to facilitate that. Spending wisely on the right players is what's kept the club so successful.'

To prove the point, signings were made: Dutch international goalkeeper Edwin van der Sar arrived from Fulham and Ji-Sung Park joined from PSV Eindhoven. Patrice Evra and Nemanja Vidić also joined the club in the January 2006 transfer window, underlining the new owners' commitment to strengthening the team.

The need to bring in new players would have been especially apparent to Ferguson in the wake of Chelsea's convincing 2004–05 league triumph. With unparalleled spending power, thanks to Roman Abramovich's huge investment in the club, Chelsea were now the team to beat. Such was their success, Ferguson was even having to contemplate the need to go the whole season without defeat in order to have a chance of usurping the Blues in 2005–06. 'The game has changed,' he said. 'We are possibly starting the Premier League saying we cannot afford to lose a game. We certainly cannot afford another slow start.'

However, before the new season had even begun, Ferguson had to deal with rumours of discontent within his squad. Just prior to United embarking upon their Far East pre-season tour, stories emerged of a clash between Fergie and Roy Keane on the training pitch at their camp in Portugal. It was alleged that Keane was unhappy that the players' wives and children had been allowed to travel with the team to the Algarve as he felt that it would distract from the preparations for the upcoming season. But any suggestion that these rumours had foundation was instantly quashed, and the reason given for Keane being left behind when United boarded the plane for Asia was a hamstring injury.

On the tour, United's first-team squad had mixed results, and Ferguson expressed concern that they were not converting all their excellent approach work into goals. 'It was a bit like the FA Cup final again,' said Fergie. 'We created a lot of chances, and the movement was good, but we were not finishing at all well. Hopefully we are not going to miss as many as that in the Champions League.' It was a statement that was to become prophecy.

The Roy Keane saga was not the only difficulty facing the club that summer. For a start, there was still the matter of Rio Ferdinand's new contract. The rumour mill went into overdrive once more, and many fans were annoyed at reports that he was holding out for £120,000 a week. United had been loyal to Ferdinand during his lengthy suspension for missing a dope test, and the supporters thought that his high wage demands showed less than a repayment of that loyalty.

Eventually, of course, it was all sorted, and Ferdinand explained that the figures that had been mentioned were in the realms of 'Fantasy Football'. 'Hopefully, now that I have signed a new contract, we can just get on with the season,' he said. 'If I had been a fan hearing all those figures knocked about, I would have reacted the same way that they did, but there was no truth in me getting such a huge offer and wanting more. Those figures were just crazy.'

Things were helped along when just a few days later Paul Scholes also signed a new contract. 'Paul has given us 16 great years of service,' Ferguson said. 'We hope his next four years are as good as his last four. He has deserved our loyalty, because he has given us plenty back.'

With John O'Shea, Darren Fletcher and Cristiano Ronaldo all about to sign on the dotted line as well, Fergie was a happy man. 'We are equally delighted Rio has signed, and with John and Darren agreeing their contracts and Cristiano probably signing his next week, we have a team that can stay together for four years now, which is fantastic news.'

The scene was set for a confident and united Red Devils to travel to Goodison Park on Saturday, 13 August 2005 for the first match of the season. Fergie knew that nothing less than a flying start would do. The previous season, United had lost their opening game to Chelsea, and, as Ferguson had pointed out, they were chasing points all season after that.

Former Red Phil Neville made his debut for Everton that day, only a week after signing for the Merseyside club for £3.5 million, and Wayne Rooney found himself playing against his former club once again. It was a cut-and-thrust match with United doing most of the thrusting, and just before half-time, Ruud van Nistelrooy popped up to round off a move by Rooney and O'Shea. United were on their way – the first goal of the season had been scored. Then, shortly after half-time, Rooney was gifted the kind of chance he simply cannot resist, and United were 2–0 ahead. That's the way it stayed, and the coach back to Manchester was a happy one. The flying start had been achieved.

United's first Premiership home game of the season was against Aston Villa, a fixture which Fergie was determined to win in order to establish some momentum after the victory against Everton. In the past, the United machine had seemed to inevitably achieve success, but it had been faltering in recent seasons, showing a hesitancy that had led to dropped points. Ferguson's rugged determination would have to come to the fore once again if further success was to be attained. He would have to prove to his critics that he was as hungry to bring trophies to Old Trafford as ever.

This hunger was shown by his team in a 1–0 win over Villa. Although the scoreline suggested otherwise, it was an emphatic performance, and United had won their first three competitive games without conceding a goal. (The third of these victories had been a 3–0 defeat of Debrecen in the first leg of United's Champions League qualifier.) Perhaps more significantly, Ruud van Nistelrooy had been on the score sheet again, three goals in three matches indicating that he was hitting form once more. 'It is important for us that Ruud scores, because once he gets on a run, he is unstoppable,' said Fergie. 'In his first season with us, he scored 36 goals. In his second, he scored 44. He is capable of doing that again this season, and that will be great for all of us.'

With qualification to Europe's major league guaranteed by a 3–0 second-leg victory in Budapest on the Wednesday after the game against Villa, the only blot on the landscape was the loss of Gary Neville for five weeks or so. He was taken off after ten minutes of the game in Hungary with a groin injury. In fact, United played the last twenty minutes of that game with only ten men after Kieran Richardson had to leave the pitch with a knee injury when United had used all their substitutes. However, Fergie remained upbeat, even with Neville sidelined: 'Losing Gary for some weeks is a blow, of course, but you have to cope with these things.'

237

At the end of August, United were away to Newcastle. They had played four competitive games and won them all, but Newcastle would provide them with another big test. At the hotel before the game, Ruud van Nistelrooy bumped into Sir Bobby Robson, who had been his boss at PSV Eindhoven. 'It was good to see him again,' said Ruud. 'He told me that it was exactly a year since he had been sacked by Newcastle, so I promised him I would score a goal for him.'

He did, too, as United won 2–0, Wayne Rooney hitting the first and Ruud the second. Fergie could not have been happier and heaped praise on his dynamic duo. He also heaped praise on his new goalkeeper Edwin van der Sar, whom he had signed at the second attempt having failed to capture him a few years earlier when Peter Schmeichel moved on to new pastures.

'It is clear for everyone to see that Edwin has made a major impact,' said Fergie at a press conference. 'His calming influence, his personality, his professionalism and his experience show through all the time.

'In Hungary for the second leg of the Champions League qualifier, we were 3–0 up on the night, 6–0 on aggregate, and he was still giving someone in defence some stick in the last minute of the game. That is a good thing. He is letting the players know what he expects from them. That is the sign of a quality goalkeeper.'

At the same time, Fergie was delighted with the transformation of Alan Smith from striker to midfield dynamo. Smith was being groomed to take over from Roy Keane eventually and even took advice from his captain. 'I want to do my best and that included taking advice from the best,' said Smith. 'Having said that, I also wanted to make it a difficult choice for the manager when he had to choose between Roy and me. I wanted to give the manager a problem.'

With three Premiership matches and a two-leg Champions League tie all successfully completed and with 11 goals scored and none conceded, things were looking very good indeed. Even those fans who had so ferociously opposed the Glazer family and their ownership of Manchester United seemed to be coming round. Life was not so bad after all. Of course, it was still very early in the season. Fergie is no fool, and he was not going to start ordering silver cleaner at that stage.

After international matches interrupted the early flow of the season, it was back to business with the Manchester derby. Fergie must have been annoyed by the international break because his players did not have the same cohesion against City, and even though they had the better of the match, they trudged off at the end of the game having conceded their first goal of the season, dropping two points in the process. City celebrated the point from their visit to Old Trafford, but United did not, and Fergie saw one of the best starts he had ever had to a season in 20 years with the Reds come to a halt.

More points were dropped a few days later, this time in the Champions League against Villarreal, for whom ex-United player Diego Forlán was now starring. The match ended in a 0–0 draw and Wayne Rooney was sent off for sarcastically applauding the referee. To make matters worse, Gabriel Heinze was also carried off with ruptured cruciate ligaments. It was a black day for United, especially when it was later revealed that Heinze, who had rapidly become a star player, would be out for the rest of the season. There was even a chance the player would miss the World Cup. 'I know how much he wants to play in the World Cup,' Ferguson said. 'But I can't see it myself. I can't see him playing before next season. I would have thought it very, very unlikely that he could be back before the end of the season.'

Although Ferguson's dark prognosis was ultimately proved to be wrong, United struggled to cope with the loss of Heinze. Mikael Silvestre had problems with a groin injury, and John O'Shea and Kieran Richardson both found it difficult to fill the boots of the Argentinian. Pressure on the manager was mounting.

The month of September passed without success. A draw at Liverpool was creditable but did not help the championship campaign, especially since skipper Roy Keane had rushed back from a hamstring injury only to break a foot during the match. Typically, Fergie kept his cool and refused to concede that Chelsea had already as good as won the title. 'It is far too early to be saying that Chelsea have won the championship,' he said. 'There are some tough games in this league, and there are games that will not be easy for Chelsea.'

A defeat at home to Blackburn made matters worse, while the possibility of United not getting past the first group stage in Europe started to become increasingly likely, even though a home victory over Benfica meant that the Reds were undefeated after two games. Ruud van Nistelrooy stabbed home the winner from close range late in the second half, but it was the uncertainty of the victory, coming as it did after the Blackburn defeat, that contributed to the feeling that United's progress to the knockout stages was far from guaranteed.

The fans had barracked Fergie during that home defeat by Blackburn and were demanding tactical changes. The boss remained unruffled, although Carlos Queiroz allegedly told the fans to be quiet in an interview with a Portuguese journalist. Mark Hughes was also quick to support his former boss after his Blackburn side won at Old Trafford. 'There are huge expectations at United,' said Hughes. 'They work with that on a day-to-day basis – they are used to it. Defeat often makes them stronger, and once they are backed into a corner, they seem to come out stronger still. It is still early days as far as the Premiership title is concerned, and it might be difficult for United to peg back Chelsea but not impossible. They are used to this kind of thing at Old Trafford.

'When you are with Manchester United, you are there to be shot at, and people fire barbed comments at you. Sir Alex has been through it many times before, and it makes him all the more determined to push words down people's mouths.'

Fergie was firing barbed comments of his own a few days later when he complained to the media about London clubs putting up their prices whenever they were at home to United. He had a point, but, more importantly, his statement demonstrated that he knew he had to strengthen his relationship with the army of United supporters. Criticism of his tenure had been growing and this calculated outburst was the boss's shrewd response to get the fans back on side.

Things were made more difficult for Ferguson at the end of the month when Roy Keane confirmed that the 2005–06 season would be his last at Old Trafford. Keane wanted to play on for another season or two but it would be at a new club. 'I think it would be good to experience a different dressing-room,' he said. 'It won't be with an English team, though. I don't think I could come back to Old Trafford and go into the away dressing-room.' The loss of the talismanic Keane would be huge, especially as he epitomised what Ferguson expected from his players. The fans would also be unhappy to see their captain leave and would be quick to vent their frustration if Fergie did not bring in a suitable replacement. The Keane situation would become increasingly complicated as the season progressed but was already causing the boss significant problems.

The ship had to be steadied, and the next port of call was Craven Cottage, where Fulham manager Chris Coleman revealed his disbelief at the criticism aimed at Sir Alex. 'If Sir Alex is booed, what hope have I got?' he said. 'He's being booed even though he's won the Champions League, FA Cups and Premiership titles. This is Alex Ferguson we are talking about. Whoever takes over from him faces the hardest job in the world. When I got the Fulham job, he was one of the first to phone me and give me some advice.'

Fulham were beaten 3–2 with van Nistelrooy scoring twice and Rooney hitting the other – the scoring machine seemed to be working again. Edwin van der Sar was less than happy about conceding two goals to his former club, but at least the points went to Manchester.

A fortnight later, the points went to Manchester again when they won 3–1 at Sunderland. Rooney and van Nistelrooy got one each, and Giuseppe Rossi announced his arrival with the third goal. But the performance was still not convincing. Fergie was upbeat, but you couldn't help feeling that he was not at peace with the way things were going.

A home draw against Tottenham continued the indifferent form. More worrying was the fact that it was Mikael Silvestre who scored United's goal: the defence had been suspect for a while, but surely the goal machine was not going to grind to a halt as well. Ronaldo scored in the next game, away to Middlesbrough, but it was a disastrous match with United conceding four goals. Speculation about Fergie's future bubbled up once again.

Meanwhile, the battle to progress from Champions League group D continued, but European competition brought no respite for Fergie's team. It seems incredible now to think that United failed to get past the group stage. The opposition had not seemed particularly daunting when the draw was made, but a few days after the drubbing at Middlesbrough, a 1–0 defeat at Lille meant that the writing was well and truly on the wall. United had only managed a 0–0 draw when they had played the French outfit at home and the Reds' position in Europe was starting to look precarious. The word 'crisis' was used in a number of newspaper headlines, but there was still a home game against Villarreal and an away match at Benfica to come. United were not really out of it when they returned from Lille, but they were not looking like the imperious, confident team of old.

However, when they drew their penultimate match against Villarreal, in which they failed to score for the third Champions League game in a row, an early exit from the competition seemed increasingly likely. It all came down to the final group match against Benfica in Lisbon. United lost 2–1 and were eliminated from Europe, coming last in their group.

On the domestic front, things were looking equally bad. The gap between themselves and runaway Premiership leaders Chelsea looked insurmountable, and the FA Cup and the Carling Cup seemed to be the only viable trophies on offer. But Fergie's team rose to the challenge and refused to concede defeat so early in the season. Of course, there was no way that a winner such as Ferguson would allow his team to roll over and die without a fight. And Fergie is never better than when he can develop a siege mentality, which is what was in place when Chelsea were visitors to Old Trafford on 6 November 2005. It was one of those rare occasions when United were underdogs on their own ground, and the United boss loved it. Darren Fletcher scored the only goal of the game, and there were smiles around the Theatre of Dreams once again.

However, it was more than just a victory over the runaway league leaders: it was a fresh start that saw United win seven and draw two of the nine Premiership games that took them to the end of 2005. The last game of the year was a 4–1 victory at home to Bolton, a great way to celebrate Hogmanay and Fergie's 64th birthday. And the return to scoring form of Ruud van Nistelrooy, who was starting to establish a great understanding with Wayne Rooney, Cristiano Ronaldo and Ryan Giggs, made it even better.

The United goal machine was starting to produce the goods again.

The scene seemed set for another Fergie miracle. Chelsea had been unconvincing in a few games, and their lead had been diminished, although they were still sitting at the top of the table. As a result, some observers started to give credence to the possibility of a Chelsea collapse, not dissimilar to Newcastle's in the 1995–96 season. United's form was good, and they looked to be well placed to capitalise should their rivals falter.

But they didn't. Chelsea stumbled but held on, and further injuries in the United camp meant that it was a bridge too far for Fergie's men. The showdown between the two teams at Stamford Bridge in April 2006 could have been the most colossal fixture of the season, but it turned out to be an anticlimax, Chelsea easily winning 3–0 and securing the championship for the second year in a row.

Perhaps if Roy Keane had still been at the club, things might have been different. However, he had been transferred to Celtic in the January 2006 transfer window after he had allegedly criticised some of his teammates on a programme for MUTV that eventually went unbroadcasted. His unstinting drive might have inspired United to pursue Chelsea with greater purpose. On the other hand, Keane's performance levels had dipped somewhat in recent years, and his injuries were becoming more frequent. It is not often that Fergie makes a mistake in the transfer market, and he would be unlikely to concede that Keane would have made a difference.

Earlier in the season, United had kissed the FA Cup farewell after a 1–0 defeat at Liverpool, but there was still the Carling Cup to fall back on and the prospect of at least something to show for the season. United progressed through the competition and made it to the final in Cardiff. Their opposition that day were Wigan Athletic, for many the surprise team of the Premiership campaign. Before the 2005–06 season began, a number of pundits had tipped

Wigan as favourites for relegation, but they had proved that they were good enough to stay among the elite. Could they pull off a surprise in the Carling Cup final as well?

Fergie knew that there was no place for second best in this match, and the end result was a convincing 4–0 victory for United. Even though the Carling Cup was at the bottom of the trophy pecking order, something positive had been salvaged from the season. However, there were those in the media who were less than gracious when their hopes of a surprise Wigan victory were denied. They concentrated instead on off-the-pitch developments – the possibility that Ruud van Nistelrooy would be leaving Old Trafford. The Dutch striker, who still ended the season as the team's top scorer despite absenteeism through injury and dips in form, seemed none too happy about sitting on the bench throughout the Carling Cup final, but he made no comment other than to say that he understood Fergie's reason for selecting Louis Saha ahead of him. But van Nistelrooy was left out of the United first team on many more occasions towards the end of the season, and his relationship with the manager seemed to have deteriorated.

Things came to a head on the final day of the season. United finished their campaign with a 4–0 victory over Charlton, confirming that they would be in the Champions League the following season without having to battle through the qualifying rounds. However, the match was overshadowed by van Nistelrooy leaving the team hotel before kick-off after having been told by Ferguson that he would not be playing. The United boss did not give much away when he spoke to Sky before the match but did say that van Nistelrooy's position would be discussed with the board. Since then, rumours about the Dutch striker's imminent departure have been rife, and it seems unlikely that he will play for United again.

With Keane gone and van Nistelrooy as good as, Ferguson has much to do in the close season. And while some observers have questioned whether or not he should call it a day and stand aside for someone else to take over as manager, the man himself has lost none of his fight. He continues to speak openly about his plans for the future and does not appear to be someone who is about to walk away from football. His statements following the injury of Wayne Rooney also demonstrate that he has both eyes on next season and intends to continue as manager of Manchester United. He was not slow to voice his opinion over the inclusion of Wayne Rooney in the England World Cup squad, and although he promised that the club would do its best to get the young star fit, he also suggested that it was putting far too much pressure on Rooney to be expected to recover from broken bones and perform at his best within a matter of weeks. The United boss made it clear that while he understood the importance of Rooney to England's World Cup hopes, he would not do anything that would jeopardise his player's fitness in readiness for the start of the next domestic season. Nothing in his words or actions has implied that he is ready to give up just yet, and it would be no surprise to see him on the touchline for the beginning of the 2006–07 season.

Epilogue

THE LEGACY CONTINUES

THE 2005–06 SEASON WAS ONE OF THE MOST DIFFICULT IN FERGIE'S LONG AND distinguished career, and it would not be surprising if he at times felt like retiring, especially as he has nothing left to prove. But the will to do it all again still burns strongly within him. He is no quitter and is unlikely to go unless it is in a blaze of glory. Everything suggests that Ferguson has no intention of leaving his beloved post any time soon.

There might come a time when Fergie believes it is time to give up football, but will he ever be able to just walk away? He knows too much and has too much energy to just slump into a favourite armchair and read the papers. You cannot stop the advancing of years, but, equally, you cannot cork passion. Fergie has always been driven by passion: a passion to achieve and a passion for football. It is his life.

From his boyhood in Govan, when the family lived in a block of tenement flats near the Clyde, football has been everything to Ferguson. He came from very ordinary beginnings, but thanks to his grit and determination, as well as a large dose of skill, he was able to transcend his background to become one of the most successful managers of all time – and was knighted along the way. His personality was shaped during these formative years, and he still displays many of the character traits that were developed at this time. It is these character traits that have made him such a formidable opponent.

But there are many facets to Sir Alex, and while we have mostly dealt with those who have positive things to say, there are also those who find it hard to speak well of him, accusing him of being unethical, ill-mannered and a bully. Whatever your view, it is clear that Ferguson is a man who is unique in the world of football. Few managers have ever masterminded their side to a Treble, as he did with Manchester United, winning everything on offer to his team except the League Cup in that one spectacular 1998–99 campaign. And it cannot be denied that he has won more trophies than almost anyone else, doing so with two different clubs in two different countries.

Although his success as a player was limited, as a manager he has gone from one brilliant success to another. For many, being appointed as manager of Aberdeen would have been the ultimate. For many more, being appointed as manager of Manchester United would have been the absolute ultimate. But not for Fergie. For him, being appointed to both jobs was just the beginning, and you get the impression that that is how he views everything. Yesterday's achievements are quickly filed away and today is a fresh start; there is no looking back and dwelling on past glories.

But a look back at his career shows that he has delivered unprecedented success at every club he has managed. True, he did not win anything with East Stirling, but he left before he had the chance to make a real impact, and the club was definitely on the up during his brief tenure. Then, he directed St Mirren to promotion and laid the foundations for the team's future success. Following this, his management of Aberdeen resulted in the most successful period in the club's history – by far. He shattered the apparently unbreakable domination of the Old Firm, winning league trophies, Scottish Cups and even the European Cup-Winners' Cup. This alone would have been enough to cement his place in the manager's hall of fame, but his legacy of success burgeoned at Manchester United. In his twenty seasons in charge, he has won a remarkable eight Premiership titles, five FA Cups, two League Cups, one European Cup-Winners' Cup, one European Cup and six Premier League Manager of the Year awards.

To be able to turn around the fortunes of more than one club and maintain a sustained period of success demonstrates that Fergie is no fluke. He has systematically and purposefully set about changing the fate of the teams he has managed and has brought his many skills and attributes to bear. He is a revolutionary, a man who has made an art form of man management, of tactics, of timing, of temper, of mind games, of selecting his players and his staff, of battling authority, of shouldering blame, of nurturing young talent, of scowling in the face of adversity and, most importantly, of winning. His preparation and attention to detail are legendary, and his knowledge of the opposition, whoever they may be, is unparalleled. But most of all, it is Fergie's single-mindedness, determination and will to win that have brought him so many trophies and records.

But his legacy to football is not just statistics in record books, however, it is an entire approach to the game. Like other great managers who have gone before him, Ferguson has bequeathed his experience and football knowledge to those who have worked with him. And let's face it, if you want to learn from someone and adapt their ideas to your own, it is better to learn from the best than one of the rest. Observing someone who has achieved what Ferguson has can only be of benefit to anyone who has had the privilege. Closely watching a master at work, studying his methods, observing what works and what fails, must be a great asset to anyone's career.

And there is quite an array of football peronalities who have worked for or alongside Fergie, including Bryan Robson, Walter Smith, Steve Bruce, Graeme Souness, Mark Hughes, Roy Keane, Alex McLeish, Gordon Strachan and Mike Phelan, among others. Some say that he taught them about man management, while others believe it is Fergie's match preparation that has had the greatest impact on them. Still others believe that it is his rugged determination to win the war even if the occasional battle is lost that they will take away from their time spent working with him. But all have one thing in common: they all learned something from Ferguson that has been of benefit to them in their own careers.

Being able to influence those around him and, as a consequence, the wider game gives Ferguson a tremendous amount of satisfaction, and he takes pride in seeing his former players gradually finding their way in coaching and management. 'It does give me great pleasure to see them moving into management,' he once said. 'I like it when they are successful because you feel that you may have helped in some small way.

'You can never really tell if a player will be a successful manager, but there are those of whom you kind of expect it. Sometimes you are surprised and the player you believe will make a good manager doesn't want to know, while others just take to it like a duck to water.

'If any of my players has learned anything from me, it is that to be a good manager you have to work really hard and have a very thick skin. Those attributes might just see you through.'

But, of course, Fergie continues to have considerable influence on the game. Until he finally closes the book on his career, he will continue to gain knowledge and experience for himself and for those with whom he comes into contact. He continues to win friends and enemies in equal measure, but, love him or hate him, nobody can argue that he has not been successful or that he hasn't changed football in this country for ever.

The football manager has an existence that is often lonely and people can be fickle, something that Sir Alex himself has acknowledged: 'You know who your friends are when the room goes dark and everybody leaves. When the light comes on and you look around, your friends are the ones still there with you.' It is a life in which you have to lose your temper regularly and fight all comers, and it is a life in which your character will be assassinated by the same people who wanted to elevate you to sainthood the day before. But it is also a life that can yield fame, fortune and the satisfaction of winning. And no one has won more than Fergie. He has had an extraordinary impact on British football and will continue to do so for many years to come. Sir Alex Ferguson's legacy to football is of immeasurable importance and only time will tell just how significant his contribution has been. But without doubt, the beneficiaries of the Fergie legacy have much to be thankful for.